Without Deadly Force

The Dynamics of Street Arrests Using

Delayed Reaction Time

Charles E. Williams

&

Dayn Derose, M.A. & Daryn Derose, PhD.

Published by:

C. E. Williams
HDI Investigation & Executive Protection Service, Inc.
P.O. Box 817
Indian Trail, North Carolina 28079
www.hdiinvestigation.com

ISBN: 978-0-9908414-1-8
ISBN: 13: 0990841413

ACKNOWLEDGEMENTS

First, I want to thank God for his mercy and goodness, as he continues to bless me and my family.

I also want to thank my wife Angela for her love, patience and encouragement.

Thanks to my children, Jordan, Logan, Taryn, Kaylin, Quentin and my grandchildren for being my inspiration. I also want to thank "G" again for being there so long ago to teach me about the streets of New York City; and my editor D. Marie Bouie, for sticking with me on this second book because we do make a great team.

Without Deadly Force

The Dynamics of Street Arrests Using

Delayed Reaction Time

Table of Contents

Prologue 8

What Is D.R.T? 10

Introduction 13

The Dynamics of Arrest 16

The Problem of Subject Containment 23

Methods of Approach (Personal Experiences) 30

The Formulation of the DRT Method 33

The Elements of Dynamic Capture 45

The Moment of Contact 57

Arrest Team Tactics and DRT 62

DRT Application to Arrest Team Tactics Examples 71

Table of Figures

Figure 1: The Arrest Perimeter and the Subject's Zone of Awareness 17
Figure 2: The Eight Directions of Approach and Escape.......................................23
Figure 3: Hypothetical Containment Perimeter with 40-Foot Radius 25
Figure 4: Containment Perimeter with 15-Foot Radius 26
Figure 5: The Sensory Motor Nerve Center of the Brain 34
Figure 6: Outline of the Human Nervous System..35
Figure 7: Adrenalin Release Triggered by a Startling Stimulus..............................36
Figure 8: Sympathetic Nervous System Stimulation Due to Startle 37
Figure 9: Outline of the Major Motor Nerve Pathways 38
Figure 10: Stages for a Surprised, Uncontrolled Subject 40
Figure 11: Typical DRT Recovery Periods for an Uncontrolled Subject............41
Figure 12: Areas of Central and Peripheral Vision..45
Figure 13: Visual Orientation to Stimulus Location and "Tip of Nose" 47
Figure 14: The Zones of Ambiguity in Human Hearing...49
Figure 15: Stimulus Distance, Field of Vision and Motion Parallax....................51
Figure 16: Hogan's Alley 65
Figure 17: Two Vehicles, Single Subject...71
Figure 18: Four Vehicles, Subject with Associates 73
Figure 19: Vehicular DRT, Two Vehicles, Single Subject 76
Figure 20: One Vehicle, Deployed Agent, Single Subject 78
Figure 21: Two Agent Arrest Tactics...80

PROLOGUE

This book encompasses the author's more than 23 years of investigative experience as a FBI Special Agent. Thirteen of those years were spent as a member of the prestigious New York City FBI Fugitive Task Force where the author's daily task consisted of locating and apprehending armed and dangerous fugitives who fled their respective states to avoid prosecution. That experience gave the author the opportunity to participate, plan and or execute more than 500 arrests as a special agent to include the arrest of at least one of the FBI's Top 10 Most Wanted Fugitives. This book was co-authored with Dayn Derose, M.A. and Daryn Derose, PhD.

This release of this book is timely, given the police shooting incidents in Ferguson, Mo., Charleston, SC, Charlotte, NC and the recent choking death in New York City, along with many other deaths where deadly force or excessive physical force was allegedly used. The purpose of this book is not to be critical of law enforcement or to take sides, when taking sides is not the answer. The answer is anchored in three pivotal areas factoring in the incidence of a favorable arrest for all parties involved. Those factors are: 1) *Training*; 2) the *Mindset* of all parties involved in the arrest; and 3) the unique *Situation* surrounding each arrest.

The purpose of this book is to provide law enforcement officers with another option; one focused on exercising proper training and the right mindset for achieving an increased level of safety for the officer and the reduction of physical force directed toward the subject. Theoretically, there would be an escalation of force starting from the request or demand for compliance. If the subject is not compliant and chooses to resist in some form or fashion, then the next level of force, physical force, becomes necessary. That involves the utilization of "personal weapons" such as hands, fists, elbows, knees, etc., to grapple with or strike the subject. Less than deadly force involves the use of stun guns, pepper spray, Tasers, batons, choke holds, etc.

Finally, there is "deadly force" wherein a gun is used to neutralize the subject and any perceived threat of danger. DRT, when used properly, displaces the subject's need to make a decision about whether to comply, thereby eliminating the escalation of force at the point of the encounter. That decision, had it been made by the subject, might have resulted in an escalation of force due to non-compliance. This book explains that not every arrest requires the use of deadly force or great physical force.

We are in an era where community policing has come to rely on the mindset that weapons and a show of force, and reliance on high capacity assault weapons and SWAT type tactics, followed by the command to "Freeze or get shot is the way to go!" This text explains how a subject can safely and effectively be arrested by using a natural, unavoidable phenomenon called, "Delayed Reaction Time (DRT)", combined with tactical team coordination and a new mindset about how to execute street arrests. This book will also explain:

- How the human body cannot avoid a DRT response to a given stimuli
- How a trained arrest team can exploit the delayed reaction in a subject
- Step-by-step illustrations on how to conduct a street arrest using DRT
- How the exploitation of DRT places officers and subjects in the safest positions
- How to properly gain physical control of the suspect
- Utilizing the environment where the arrest is taking place…and much more.

The author has put the reader right on the street with the arrest team, offering a front-row seat into the mind of the arresting agent and the subject of the arrest.

WHAT IS D.R.T?

DRT (Delayed Reaction Time) is systematic use of the reactions a subject always has, when confronted properly, during a planned street arrest. DRT makes use of human perceptual flaws, which can be provoked when a subject is approached from specific angles.

Q: Aren't we discussing the "element of surprise"?
A: DRT is more than the element of surprise, but certainly includes it. DRT is a method of producing a certain type of surprise and exploiting it. A planned, innocuous, approach into close quarters with the subject will produce a physical reaction which can be used to control the subject's behavior at the moment of arrest. This reaction is a sort of freeze/startle reaction. Mere surprise by itself, is much less reliable than DRT.

Q: Why does DRT specify a street arrest? Why not elsewhere?
A: DRT techniques are drawn from practical experience, not merely "drawing board" science. They are not meant for every scenario. These techniques were developed (and used) for years in order to handle arrests where:

- Subject's residence could not be located.
- Subject's location was difficult to predict at any given time.
- Residential data was limited to the subject's outside activities and habits.
- Arresting agents received notification of the subject's location or residence, and an immediate arrest was necessary.

Q: What about armed subjects?
A: DRT methods always proceed from the assumption that the subject is armed and dangerous. One of the reasons for the development of DRT was to enable agents to make an arrest before the subject recovered from the surprise of being "stopped" and could possibly decide to "go for it" by introducing a weapon.

One of the most important aspects of a DRT arrest is visual affirmation that the subject does not have a weapon in hand. If the subject has a weapon in hand (i.e. is anticipating an immediate arrest), the situation is not within the scope of a DRT type action.

Q: What about a hostage situation?
A: The whole concept of DRT is to prevent the subject from being both mentally certain and physically ready to make the organized conscious decision to take a hostage. When DRT is used, bystanders are also in a much safer position. When the alternative "take cover and yell" (our term: "Stand and Deliver!") approach is used the innocent bystander may well become the most endangered person in the arrest!

Q: Be realistic, aren't the arresting agents going to have to cover the subject with their weapons?
A: A more realistic and disturbing eventuality would be having to physically control and handcuff a subject while holding a handgun in your hand. The actual approach should be made by agents who have their hands free. The other agents on the team should ready their weapons and cover the subject.

Q: Does an agent need to be a skilled "martial artist" in order to use DRT?
A: No. Although an agent already knows that every technique which pertains to physical arrest is derived from some form of martial arts. The explanation for why DRT works may seem complex, but in the end, all it requires is to grab the subject's arm and pull down, or towards an obstruction.

Q: In that case, aren't there enough arrest/control and "come-along" techniques already?
A: DRT is not a collection of favorite arrest/control-come-along techniques. If DRT is correctly applied, the arresting agent won't need more extreme or painful measures to secure compliance. If, in the event a come-along is needed, DRT methods puts the agent in the best possible position to apply a more extreme physical restraint, at the best possible time.

Q: Is this a more "humane" method of arrest, in that it refrains from the use of weapons, deadly force, come-along and or the perception or reality of police brutality at the expense of the agent's safety?
A: That is not the intent of the DRT method. DRT is more "humane" to the subject, but that is a beneficial byproduct of DRT's efficiency when it is used properly. DRT isn't an idea yet to be tested. It was systematized after an extensive examination of successful street arrests by the author.

The most effective tactics were kept and refined. The less efficient aspects of standard arrests, many of which were dangerous for the agents, were eliminated. The research of this book was an effort to identify why subjects invariably exhibited the reactions they did when arrested in the DRT manner.

DRT is a strategy for taking advantage of these mental and physical reactions, which occur, to some degree, in every subject. Although it is more "humane" than "combative," the sole intent is to be efficient.

Q: Must an arresting agent always put hands on the subject to achieve a successful use of DRT?
A: Not always. There is a "no hands" DRT method applicable to specific scenarios; particularly, vehicular approach. These scenarios are explained in the text.

Q: If the approach is to be apparently innocuous, is it necessary for the arrest team to dress down in order to blend in with the location?
A: Not necessarily; although it is important that the subject is not aware of the arresting agents' intentions, whether the agents, themselves, are seen or not is only relatively important, depending on the situation. If the arrest is a swift one, the agents may not be on location long enough for their clothing to give them away.

INTRODUCTION

Consider, just for a moment, the potential risks of performing an arrest; taking away an unwilling person's freedom. Picture the individual as a 24-year-old male who stands six feet tall, and weighs 190lbs. Furthermore, he has an extensive criminal record; is regarded as armed and dangerous; is completely nocturnal in his activities; has no known address; and, when his whereabouts are known, he is circulating entirely in environments known to be hostile to law enforcement. This is a street arrest. It's not only difficult, it is outright dangerous and this is a typical arrest scenario for any violent crime squad.

The individual just described could star in anyone's worst nightmare. What will scare you the most is that at the time of any arrest, you can never be exactly sure how the subject will react to the realization that you are about to take away his freedom. Yes, yours is an extremely difficult job. It was the author's job too for more than two decades.

I had been a special agent for the Federal Bureau of Investigation for more than 23 years. I worked on the New York City FBI fugitive Task Force Squad for nearly 13 years. During that time, I had been involved in over 600 arrests. I can vividly recall my earliest days working on the fugitive squad. I was amazed by its proficiency and the speed and coordination with which its arrest team members executed street arrests. An extremely high percentage of those arrests were performed precisely and efficiently; as smoothly as they had been planned; even with the glitches inherent in trying to plan arrests with so many unknown variables involved. On occasion, a few of those arrests did not go smoothly. Nevertheless, they were still executed without serious injury to anyone.

As I gained experience with arrest procedures, I became fascinated with the conditions determining the outcome of an arrest. I began to search for the necessary and essential elements for a successful street arrest. I pondered whether a successful arrest was a matter of planning, training, luck or just street experience based on trial and error. Was it some combination of these, and if so, in which of these factors did the emphasis lay? In a roughly performed or unsuccessful street arrest, was some vital element missing or was the difficulty just a "tough break" or a function of the law of averages?

My discussions with other agents produced meaningful insights about the comparative effectiveness of street arrests. Their observations confirmed that planning, training, experience, and yes, sometimes a degree of luck, were essential components of a successful arrest. While I found this anecdotal information personally useful, it lacked a coherent theory grounded in the scientific method of why an arrest went smooth and why it was successful. What happens when a subject is arrested without incident? My goal was to identify scientifically, the definite, detailed, methods and guiding principles that could be subjected to empirical verification. I wanted to show, conclusively, that there was an unchanging factor, a constant in every arrest, regardless of who was being arrested.

I knew from my experience that the answers lay in the consistent appearance of a surprising phenomenon. It occurred whenever my squad executed an arrest plan with a high degree of coordination. One or more of the squad members would close in suddenly and unexpectedly. Whether that meant walking or driving up to him...the subject would *never resist*. The meanest, most vicious offenders imaginable; people who had reputations for being wolves among sheep, acted more like rabbits. Because of this subdued reaction, very little force or violence was actually needed to make the arrest. The approach we used created a momentary window of opportunity for the arresting agent; during which the agent was in the safest position and the subject was in the most vulnerable position. I realized that this invariably recurring event was the element I had been looking for; a "constant" in the equation of a successful arrest with the least amount of resistance, force and or incidents.

Once I realized that this "moment of vulnerability" existed, the next step was to ascertain the factors producing it so it could be reproduced regularly and at the agent's will.

It became clear that the reasons for the squad's consistent success on the street were anchored in the arrest team's deliberate manipulation of the physiological factors controlling a subject's ability to react and resist arrest. The subject had to be approached in a sudden, unexpected manner, after the agents had formed a pre-planned surrounding known as a "sphere of containment."

To the best of my knowledge, up until the present, no text existed that provided cogent theory, quantifiable data, and practical instruction relative to the dynamics driving the ultimate success or failure of a street arrest. Because of the continued influx of drugs and gangs and the resulting dramatic escalation of violence on our streets, this lack of instruction has become an increasingly dangerous omission pertaining to the safety of law enforcement officers and results in the unnecessary use of too much force.

Back when we were fighting what I called the, "Crack War" in New York City, law enforcement officers were literally deployed to a battle ground. Stress was extremely high and nerves were sometimes too short. Because of this, law enforcement officers should possess knowledge and training in any methodology that gives them the slightest advantage. Law enforcement has made tremendous investments in forensic science, psychological profiling, SWAT teams and tactics, and in procuring weapons and ammunition offering the greatest stopping power. While research in these fields is of a driving urgency, the law enforcement community has yet to effectively commit its resources to an equally urgent need---in depth analysis of the safest, most effective way to execute a street arrest.

This text presents a systematic approach using insights drawn from empirical research, street experience, and martial arts training (particularly judo), to identify the dynamics determining the outcome of any street arrest. These phenomena will be examined and clearly explained. The methods capitalizing on this phenomena will be explained, through both general discussion and case examples, how they can be successfully learned, adopted and utilized by every law enforcement officer.

The basis of this approach to arrest procedures is a thorough knowledge and deliberate manipulation of specific physiological phenomenon referred to as, "Delayed Reaction Time" (hereafter referred to as DRT). This entire approach to arrest dynamics is called the "**DRT System**."

This book explains why and how DRT occurs and how it can be an asset to law enforcement. Secondly, techniques to induce, and to prolong the DRT condition are identified. Thirdly, we shall present effective ways to utilize the DRT effect in the framework of a coordinated team effort by first surrounding the subject in a sphere of containment, then making the actual contact and arrest, while the DRT effect is still acting against the subject.

THE DYNAMICS OF ARREST

The DRT System is based upon the study of the phenomenological sphere surrounding the subject of an arrest and the subject's range of possible reactions within it. As in any planned arrest, when using DRT, the lead arresting officer and members of the arrest team should first, if possible, be well aware of the criminal history and subject's propensity for violence and/or escape. If possible, the lead arresting officer and/or the arrest team should be familiar with the layout of the area where the arrest will take place. This information will assist the lead officer in making a determination of the number of agents/officers required and the firepower and the level of intensity required to execute the arrest.

As stated above, the DRT approach views the subject of an arrest as being at the center of a sphere, or for the sake of simplicity, a circular perimeter. The subject could be standing at a street corner or against a wall. He or she could be walking in a crowded mall, or in an unpopulated area. The subject could be exiting or entering an automobile. Wherever the subject is, he or she is at the center of a personal zone of potential awareness, which has a circular perimeter.

For example, assume that an arresting team of agents has moved into position around a subject who is standing in a relatively uncluttered environment. Having posted the appropriate guards and observers, the remainder of the team surrounds the subject in order to cut off avenues of escape. The distance between any one agent and the subject can now be depicted as a radius, extending from the edge of this circle (the agent's location), to the subject's position at the center. See this configuration illustrated in Figure 1.

Figure 1: The Arrest Perimeter and the Subject's Zone of Awareness

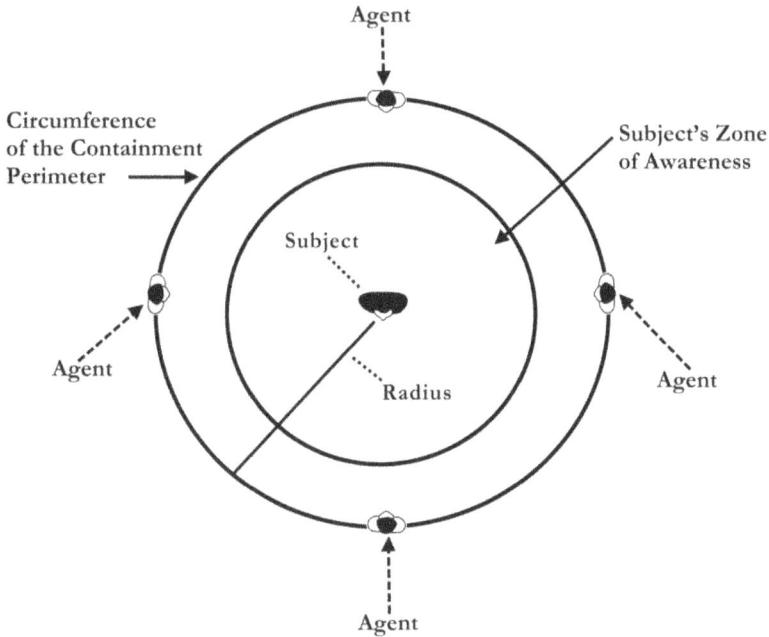

The area within the circle represents the total amount of space available to the subject in which to find an avenue of escape. Simply put, one or more of the agents must reduce the length of the radius to zero in order to effect the arrest (i.e. eliminate the space between them; close-in).

At some point during this approach-containment-arrest process, perhaps as the actual arrest is attempted, the encroaching threat will enter the subject's zone of awareness. If the subject is given sufficient time to assess the situation, the likelihood of an escape attempt or retaliatory response will be greatly increased. Therefore, in order to successfully reduce the radius to close in effectively, the subject's zone of awareness must be penetrated in a manner that will prevent the subject from making a well formed response to the threat of arrest. Parallels to this view of containment and arrest can be found in a study of the staking behaviors of predatory animals. In a recent collection of articles on ecological perception and motion, Reed (1988, chap. 13 pp 372-376), specifies three general rules for successful predation, which is the biological interaction between a predator and his prey. Based upon Reed's presentation, three principles for predation or capture are shown below:

Interception: Upon the first clear sight of prey, predatory animals will begin their approach at an acceptable rate; that is, at a rate which allows for a reasonably rapid approach to staking distance, but is not so fast that the predator cannot keep an accurate fix on the location of the prey, or so fast that the prey becomes alarmed by the motion. Predatory behavior by coordinated pack animals also involves the systematic placement of pack members so as to unobtrusively cut off possible avenues of escape.

Staking: At close range, hunting animals will typically use available cover, body movements, and postures to give only minimal evidence of their presence, while approaching in a relatively slow, direct, but non-alarming manner to get within the optimal striking distance of the intended prey.

Striking: Attacking animals will complete the approach by making sudden, often explosive, but coordinated motions to gain a position from which the prey can be readily caught.

In the last critical moments of the strike, a tidal wave of sensory information is processed by both predator and prey. The predator has carefully arranged the location, direction, position, and timing of the attack; is fully aware of the surroundings and can effectively make split-second adjustments to changes in conditions. If the prey animal has truly been taken unaware, it has no hope of making sense of these drastic changes in its sphere of awareness, and can make no directed response to the attack. More importantly, the physiological reaction to the sudden recognition of a close threat, combined with their lack of accurate information about the nature of the threat will often cause a biological overload. This will render the prey animal incapable of any timely response at all. This sensory, neurological, and hormonal overload is the animal equivalent of the DRT principle.

Case In Point #1: "He Shot a Police Officer"

In this one particular case, there was an incident that happened in New Jersey, where a young man ended up in a struggle with a police officer who had asked him to move. During the struggle, the young man, who in this story we will call, "Obadiah," was able to take the police officer's gun from him and shoot him in the chest at point blank range and then run away. The officer was wearing a ballistic garment and survived the shooting without serious injury. I talked about this story in several of the books that I have written, but I had never told the story of how Obadiah was actually physically arrested.

When the case was assigned to me, I asked my best informant, "G" to help me find Obadiah. G had a remarkable talent and track record for finding people and he was just as remarkable in finding Obadiah. G had managed somehow to get Obadiah's cell phone number and had been talking to Obadiah for about a week; gaining his trust and his confidence that G could get him out of the trouble he was in with the cop shooting. He had told Obadiah that he could arrange a meeting between him (Obadiah) and a high-profile civil rights activist who lived in Brooklyn, New York. This well-known activist would listen to his side of the story and then decide if he was willing to broker negotiations between Obadiah and the New Jersey prosecutor's office. Obadiah believed enough of this story to arrange to meet G.

The meeting was supposed to take place on Wednesday at 1:30 PM at the corner of Flatbush Avenue and Avenue U, near the Kings Plaza Mall in Brooklyn. Obadiah was supposed to stand in front of a liquor store located on that corner, directly across from a Texaco gas station.

Now, there were some lengthy discussions about how to execute the arrest. The squad supervisor was concerned because, since Obadiah had "shot a police officer," he had already shown a willingness to physically resist arrest, disarm and actually shoot a police officer. He would more than likely be armed at the time of the arrest. He also made the point that he was a flight risk because he had already fled one shooting incident, having gone from New Jersey to New York. He asked whether there was any way we could arrest him at his home. I told him we didn't know where Obadiah lived and he was constantly moving from one place to another. If we took a chance to hit one of those addresses and we missed him, we might never see him again.

My supervisor at that time wanted us to use the slow methodical approach of seeking cover and shouting commands for the subject to freeze, get down on the ground and ask him to wait three minutes for us to walk over and handcuff him. I told my supervisor that we have been practicing some new techniques based on getting as close as we could to a subject and then use team coordination, speed, the element of surprise and the opportunity it gave us to gain control of the subject. I told him to trust me and the team and we would arrest Obadiah before Obadiah even knew he was arrested.

Wednesday came. It was a beautiful day to make an arrest. The sun was out in all its glory backed up by a wonderful blue sky and not a single cloud was present. Before our squad executed an arrest, we would stage (meet) approximately forty-five minutes to one hour before the arrest. The stage time was determined by the size and complexity of the arrest. We would meet some distance, not too far, not too close, from the actual planned location of the arrest to discuss the arrest, get familiar with the area, review the plan and give out the assignments.

I made sure each agent drove past the planned location of the arrest and took note of the layout of the street and all the landmarks in the immediate area and at least one block in either direction, leading away from the corner of Flatland Avenue and Avenue U. The plan was as follows: the team was made up of 10 agents and one informant. With regard to weapons, eight agents carried handguns, and two agents were carrying shoulder weapons (shotguns). Concerning vehicles, we used one cargo van with rear and side doors containing five agents, including the driver. The following car #1 contained two agents; car #2 contained two agents and car #3 contained one agent and the informant.

Our strategy was for G to call Obadiah and keep him on the phone. Once G was able to establish Obadiah's exact location, he would advise the arrest team via radio. Once the arrest team had a visual and could see Obadiah standing in front of the liquor store, we would send in two dressed down agents who would appear to be going into the liquor store, but who would put "hands on" Obadiah. The plan for using the liquor store and the adjoining building as obstructions were for containment purposes; cutting off the subject's possible escape to the rear. A team in the cargo van would coordinate and time their approach to arrive just as the two agents were putting "hands on" Obadiah. They would exit the van and come straight at Obadiah as an additional distraction to cover Obadiah and set up an inside perimeter around him.

Cars #1 and #2 were to move at the same time, on opposites flanks, toward the subject to cover any possible escape routes, control the outside perimeter and hold back all pedestrians.

Sounded like a pretty good plan to me, so what could possibly go wrong? Well, the plan was set. The staging was completed. Let's lock and load! Let's holster up and show up! Remember the 4 C's?

1. Containment
2. Subject is the Center Of the Circle
3. Induce Confusion
4. Gain Control

Let's Rock & Roll. The arrest team members took up their positions of concealment by melting in with the surrounding community and going unnoticed, while waiting for G to make contact with Obadiah.

At one o'clock, G called Obadiah and asked him if he had arrived at the liquor store. Obadiah said, "No" but also said he was on his way. Fifteen minutes later, G called him again. Obadiah said he was on his way and would be there shortly and asked G where he was standing. G told him he was standing near the liquor store, leaning against a white car. G then advised the arrest team via radio that he thought Obadiah was somewhere in the area checking out the layout and trying to determine whether he was walking into a trap. G then stated he could see a guy standing at the Texaco gas station across the street from the liquor store, who appeared to fit Obadiah's description but he wasn't absolutely sure it was him and didn't want to get too close and spook him. So, G said he was going to hang up the phone and call Obadiah right back and see if the guy standing at the gas station took out his phone to answer. G called and he saw the guy standing at the gas station put his phone to his ear and say, "Hello?"

Street plan "A" was no longer viable. We had to switch to plan "B". We would drive the van up into the gas station as though we were pulling into the station to get some gas; with the hope of getting within 10 ft. of Obadiah. We were going to use car #1 and #2 to flank Obadiah's right and left: add to his distraction; set up an outside perimeter; cut off all avenues of escape; cover Obadiah; and give support where needed. The five agents in the van would:

Agent #1 - Driver would blend in with traffic speed and conditions; getting the van within 10 ft. of the subject. An agent can cover 10 ft. in less than 1.5 seconds. His second responsibility is to place the van in park and rapidly exit the van two seconds after agents #3, #4 and #5 exited the van. Agent #1's handgun is drawn, covering Obadiah's left flank, and establishes an inside perimeter, cutting off avenues of escape.

Agent #2 - Rapidly exits the rear of the van two seconds after Agents #3, #4 and #5 exit the van. His shoulder weapon is drawn, covering Obadiah's right flank, and establishes an inside perimeter, cutting off avenues of escape.

Agents #3, #4 and #5 - These three agents are acting in unison and are the first to exit the van:

- Agent #3: Moves and gets into position first, heading straight at Obadiah and is pointing a big shotgun in his face shouting, "FBI!! Don't move." For Obadiah, that was the equivalent of someone jumping out of the dark and saying, "Boo!"!

- Agent #4: Moves to the subject's immediate right; his weapon is <u>not</u> drawn; his purpose is to gain physical contact as quickly as possible, and then control of Obadiah. Both hands are required to do this.

- Agent #5: Moves to Obadiah's immediate left; his weapon is drawn. As he is moving toward Obadiah, he is making a decision, within one to two seconds, as to whether to holster his weapon or assist Agent #4 in the physical control and handcuffing of Obadiah.

We rolled up on Obadiah and executed the arrest just as described above. When we came out of that van, Obadiah's eyes got so big I thought they were going to pop out of his head. His mouth fell open and hung there. His feet never moved and he couldn't even talk. We were on him so fast, I had to take the phone out of his hand and say, "Goodbye" to G. From the time we exited the van, approximately 3.5 seconds later, Obadiah was in handcuffs.

THE PROBLEM OF SUBJECT CONTAINMENT

The concept of the circle of containment, formed by the sum of all the possible avenues of motion (and escape) available to the subject, is derived from principles used in many systems of personal combat (Faker, 1986; Westbrook and Ratty, 1970). For example, the basic theory of the martial art of judo specifies eight fundamental directions in which an opponent can be unbalanced and thrown. Consequently, there are eight directions in which an opponent can escape being thrown (Kano, 1986). This is illustrated below:

Figure 2: The Eight Directions of Approach and Escape

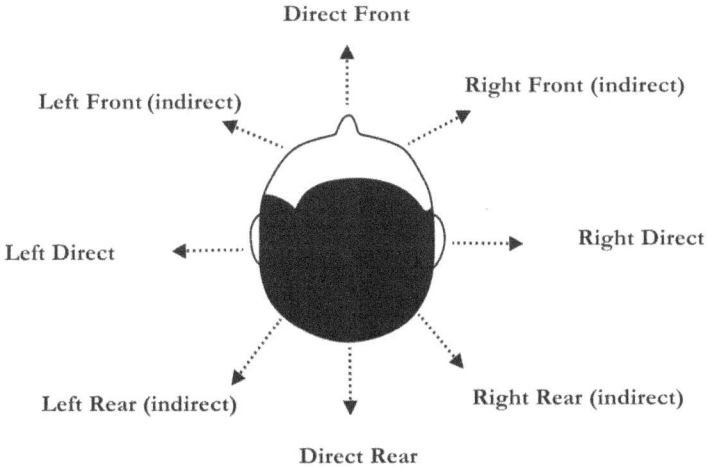

This phenomenon is applicable to the problem of containment within the sphere

Understanding this phenomenon aids in addressing the problem of containment within the sphere of an arrest. The above diagram clearly illustrates the eight minimum angles for an effective escape from an immediate, close-range confrontation. Beyond this range of immediate confrontation, where there is a larger circle of containment, there will be a greater number of angles for escape. In order to effectively contain the subject, the arrest team must be able to cover those avenues of escape. As an extreme example, if the circumference in question is as large as a city block, one hundred agents would probably be required to contain a single subject.

Before making calculations that are based upon these numbers, it is important to have a realistic idea of human running speed and reaction times. Surprisingly, most people are not aware of how much distance an individual can cover in a few seconds. For example, an average high school running back can cover 120 ft. in less than five seconds. A world class sprinter can cover 35 ft. in less than one second. It is reasonable to assume that most agents, in good condition, can cover 15 to 20 ft. in less than 3.5 seconds; approximately 5 ft. per second.

Armed with this information, it is possible to make reasonable estimates of the number of personnel required for specific containment situations. For example, assume the running speed of the agents is about 5 ft. per second and that the running speed of the subject is twice that or 10 ft. per second. Assume the terrain of the staging area makes necessary a circle of containment with a 40 ft. radius, and there are no useful environmental obstructions, such as buildings, fences or walls. Since the subject is capable of running the distance from the center of the circle of containment to its perimeter in four seconds, the agents will be placed around the perimeter at intervals of 20 ft. so no agent needs to run more than 10 ft. or more than two seconds to intercept a possible breach in his or her assigned section of the perimeter. This provides a very generous two-second margin of safety for the response times of each agent. That is, provided no agent leaves his or her assigned section of the perimeter except to assist an adjacent agent who has already intercepted the subject. With a radius of 40 ft., the perimeter of the circle of containment is 40 x ^ (approximately 3.14), or about 120 ft. Since it was decided that the agents should be posted at 20 ft. intervals, six agents would be required to contain a subject. See Figure 3.

Figure 3: Hypothetical Containment Perimeter with 40-Foot Radius

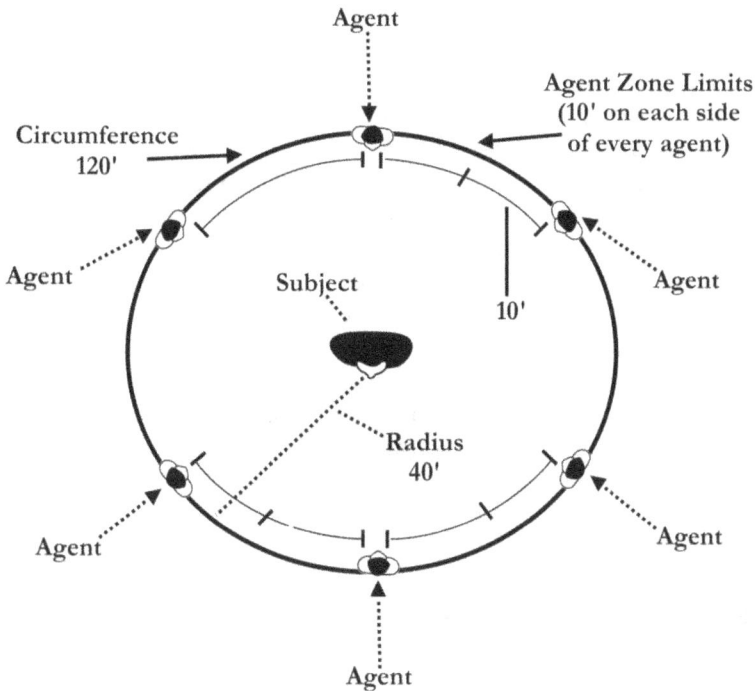

The scenario outlined above provides a convenient arrangement for the arrest team, because they will have plenty of time to react to changes in the subject's behavior. However, it must be remembered that subject containment is not the same as subject capture. In order to capture the subject, the encircling agents now face the same 40 ft. distance barrier that the subject would were he or she to attempt an escape. In that scenario, having estimated the speed of the agents at about 5 ft. per second, it appears that a running agent might take about six seconds to reach the subject. Under combat situations, this can be a very long time, during which the subject's behavior can become dangerously unpredictable. Something more seems to be needed or, literally something less, relative to the amount of time the subject has available to him before an agent can make contact with him.

If the radius of the circle of containment can be reduced to 15 ft., and the running speeds of the agents and of the subject remained constant, four agents could be posted at 12 ft. intervals to contain the subject. This would provide a small (3.25 seconds) but useful margin of safety. Using more than four agents at this range would increase the effective response time margin of safety for each agent, but at this distance, this strategy would also increase the likelihood of assignment conflicts, collisions, and dangerous crossfire.

In this second example, the avenues of escape are reduced in number because the radius, and therefore the circle of containment's perimeter, has been reduced. As in the 40 ft. example, the direction of any potential openings in the perimeter will always lie directly between any two agents.

Even in the unlikely event that none of the agents close with the subject during the execution of the arrest, any attempt at escape would bring the subject within 6 ft. of one of the agents, readily allowing for interception. Of course, the subject's propensity for violence and/or escape should also be a factor in determining the total number of agents utilized in the arrest. With a 15 foot radius, a running agent now has three seconds to traverse the distance and close with the subject at the center. This is still a long time, but at this range, a stealthy approach could be reasonably employed to bring an agent into immediate striking distance.

Figure 4: Containment Perimeter with 15-Foot Radius

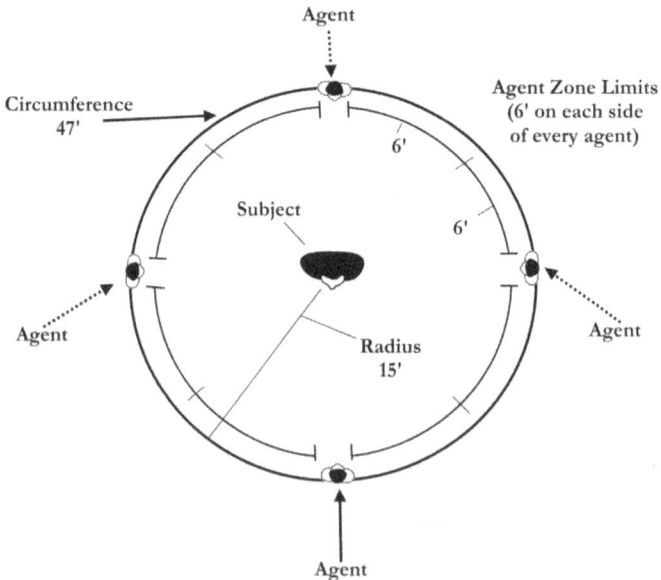

It is vitally important to understand the reasons for maximizing the smallest possible manageable area of containment. The lessening of the allowable reaction time-safety margins, which accompanies a decrease in the startling range of the agents, can have the appearance of a contradiction of the DRT premise. It may appear that the closer the agent gets to the subject, the less time they will have to react to the subject's response. This is certainly the logic behind older arrest procedures (e.g. Remsberg, 1986) which, in comparison, are based upon a kind of "stand and deliver" approach. That familiar strategy involves an enforced perimeter, and a slow, cautious approach to the subject. I am deliberately using the phrase "stand and deliver" here, to describe this older method of arrest procedures. It was the defiant challenge made by the main character in Henry Wadsworth Longfellow's famous poem "The Highwayman" as he stood in the road, blocking the progress of a horse drawn carriage.

Although it is unlikely that real felons of that era actually stood out in the open in such a fashion, variations of this tactic were actually used, in bygone times, to commit highway robbery. Of course, this method of robbery fell out of fashion, because repeating firearms became more common and many of the highwaymen that used it were shot by well-armed coachmen and passengers. In short, allowing the victims to make a considered response, resulted in disaster for the robbers. This comparison has a hard moral to its story.

Unquestionably, containment perimeters and other safeguards are essential in arrest tactics. The continued use of these precautions is emphatically advocated here. However, the purpose of this book proposes that the pattern of action and reaction in the standard arrest model or scenario should be revised. Use of the DRT System can greatly lessen the danger to both arresting officer and subject. The proper use of its well-planned, swift, and dynamic tactics deprives an arrest subject of the ability to initiate coherent actions or decisions. As will be explained below, when using the DRT System, *closer is better.*

Case In Point #2: "A Matter of Containment"

It was another beautiful day and we had an arrest plan wherein we thought the arrest was going to take place at the subject's residence. As usual, the arrest didn't go as planned. We arrived at the address in question and without giving ourselves away, we determined that the subject, who we will call Timothy, was not home; but, we were able gather information that he would be returning later that day.

Now, here's the question: Do we arrest Timothy on the street or do we let him get in the house and arrest him there? In my humble opinion, based on over 20 years of making arrests and more than thirty years of investigative experience, I had come to the conclusion that there are three major types of arrest:

- Street arrest wherein the arrest is conducted on the street
- Vehicular arrest wherein the subject of the arrest is inside a vehicle
- Enclosed arrest wherein the subject of the arrest is located inside a building

During my career, I conducted all of the above and in other places and situations as well. Each type of arrest has its own advantages and disadvantages. Given that, I would rather make an arrest on the street. I feel there are more variables I can control on the street and therefore, more advantages; but, there is a major concern about containment if the arrest is not well-planned, executed and any disadvantages addressed.

We were subsequently able to gather additional information that the subject was not expected to return until three or four hours later. So, we decided it would be better if got back into our cars and drove back to the staging area to regroup. While on our way, guess who we saw pop up, seemingly out of nowhere? Timothy. He had just come around the corner as we were walking toward him, "five deep" with guns and shields, only approximately 60 to 70 ft. away. This is the funny part: Timothy saw us as clear as you see this open book in front of you. His facial expression said it all. He was startled! To him, we appeared unexpectedly and suddenly out of nowhere!

His expression was so familiar and similar to the ones I've seen written across the faces of so many subjects. His eyes got really big, as though they would never stop growing. His mouth fell open, and he stood perfectly still; frozen in time, space, and in my memory. His gaze fixated on us for at least two to two and a half seconds; as if his mind was stuck in a trance and he couldn't escape it, no matter how hard he tried. To put it simply, he was very surprised! He simply wasn't expecting us, but he knew who we were the moment he saw us and he knew what we wanted. We wanted him!

Now, it gets even more interesting because we came there looking for him but we weren't expecting to see him come out of nowhere and just walk around the corner right in front of us. So you had five trained and experienced agents including myself just standing there, eyes big, mouths hanging open, looking straight ahead; standing perfectly still; transfixed on Timothy; unable to move for at least two seconds. Then after those two seconds, I could actually see through Timothy's eyes that his mind was beginning to clear away the clouds as he began to actively process, in *real time* the situation he was walking into. I could see him begin to figure out possible avenues of escape; measuring in his mind's eye the distances separating him from us. I could see his eyes finally move from us to look around, as he considered his situation and his options; as he tried to determine what to do. Then he was gone; running in the opposite direction, at top speed.

There was no containment. No established center or circle. The confusion was there, but both parties were startled and both parties where momentarily stuck in a state of confusion. Timothy made his own decision before we could make ours and he took the opportunity given to him, while we were caught in a phenomenon we could not escape in time to act. There was no planned DRT inducement, or a system of containment to prolong and take advantage of Timothy's confusion and without containment, there can be no subsequent control.

METHODS OF APPROACH (PERSONAL EXPERIENCES)

Now, that the stage is set within the circle of the arrest, we shall consider the crucial element of approach within this area. The question is, which is the best approach? Should it go "slow and easy" or "fast and hard"? Should the agents utilize a vehicular or on-foot approach? Should they wear raid jackets or dress down? Do they need to get close enough to put hands on the subject? Or, do they need to get to cover, some distance away, and shout, "FBI or NYPD hands up! Don't move! "

The object of the approach advocated here, is not only to shorten the radius of the circle of containment, but to induce a startle response that will cause a DRT effect in the subject. This idea of approach, coordinated with DRT, took shape in my mind when I realized that every time my arrest team successfully executed the seizure of a suspect at close quarters, the subject would always freeze, give no resistance, and would consistently adopt a genuinely confused and surprised expression wherein the subject became virtually docile! Understand that, I didn't read about this reaction. I saw it firsthand with my own eyes, over and over again. I experienced this reaction so much and found it so interesting that I began to actually take notes of what I was experiencing on the streets of New York City. I wanted to understand why it was happening and then systematize it so that the reaction was a constant in our arrests so we could take advantage of it whenever the opportunity arose.

Case In Point #3: "The Hallway"

A striking example of this behavior once occurred when my partner and I were preparing to make an arrest. The arrest team had been instructed to report to a staging area at 5:30 am on the day of the arrest. My partner and I got there earlier than 5:30 am to reconnoiter the apartment building where the arrest would take place. We expected the subject, whom we will call Immanuel, to be in his girlfriend's apartment sleeping. At one point in our reconnaissance, my partner was in the lobby and I was on the second floor, in a hallway near the subject's apartment. I was making sure I knew the hallway layout and the exact location of the subject's apartment, which was apartment #235, a number I will never forget.

As I walked past his apartment, confirmed the apartment number, and location, I continued to walk down the hallway thinking. I looked up and to my surprise, Immanuel, who was considered armed and dangerous, came walking up the stairs and down the hall. He was coming directly toward me.

I began walking toward Immanuel and I knew that if he had even an *inkling* that I was a "cop" he wouldn't have been there when I and the team came back for him. I knew I had to do something. I continued to walk toward him in a casual, nonchalant manner. I knew Immanuel knew that I didn't live there, so I knew he was a little uncomfortable with seeing me in the hallway. But, I also knew he wasn't sure whether I was an "enemy" or just someone he didn't know. All I had to do was keep him from arriving at a conclusion before I got close enough to help him make that decision.

Still walking, I came parallel to his right shoulder and quickly but calmly grabbed his right wrist with my left hand, placed my right hand on his chest, moved to his right and simultaneously pushed him calmly against the wall, so as to not initiate an automatic fight or flight response and to reduce his avenues of escape. I advised him, in a stern, but calm voice, that he was under arrest and should not move. I then called for my partner and he appeared almost immediately, and placed handcuffs on the subject. From the time I grabbed his wrist and my partner arrived on the scene, no more than two and a half seconds transpired. For the subject, it was like I jumped out of the wall and said, "Hey You!" The subject's facial expression mirrored that of Obadiah and Timothy. He offered no resistance, was visibly shaken, confused and was totally ineffective. He could neither run nor fight.

Based on seeing so many similar reactions and particularly the one I just described, I was convinced that, provided the agent's movements were truly sudden and surprising, the subject would always experience a moment when he was completely ineffective. Given these premises, the subject's startle condition was simply inescapable.

After this experience and in the majority of our street arrests, we (the arrest team) would attempt to blend in with the surrounding environment, make an approach on foot to within four or five feet of the subject, and at that distance, make a sudden move to seize the subject. The initial contact with the subject would be firm and controlling; but relatively calm and nonviolent, thus increasing the subject's confusion about the nature of the event.

Typically, control of the subject would be achieved by grabbing the subject's right wrist, while placing a hand on the back of his or her shoulder. This grip would be used to redirect and pull the subject in a circular motion, face-first to the floor or toward a wall; while advising that he or she was under arrest. At that point, other agents would move in simultaneously and handcuffs were employed. We found that without exception, if we could get to within four to five feet of the subject, we could subdue the subject before any response could be made against our motions. I also found that this period of the subject's ineffectiveness could be induced during a vehicular arrest as long as the lead, unmarked vehicle approach was performed in a non-alarming manner, and could get within 10 to 12 ft. of a subject.

Eventually, through repeated trials and using this method in actual street arrests, I confirmed that if the subject was approached unexpectedly by, or surprised by some stimuli that did not create an automatic flight response, the subject's reaction time would be reliably delayed. I also realized that the period of DRT (delayed reaction time) is of great significance to law enforcement. However, I knew that in order to present these findings, I needed to thoroughly identify and document the essential conditions for the onset of this phenomenon and its effects, in a scientific format.

THE FORMULATION OF THE DRT METHOD

The Physiology of DRT

In attempting to systematize this method, what first came to my mind was judo. Judo teaches the maximum efficient use of mental and physical energy. A judoist attempts to unbalance his or her opponent, thereby functionally reducing the opponent's strength. This allows a smaller player to throw down a much larger one. However, it is often very difficult to unbalance a larger, skilled opponent. Therefore, the judoist attempts to take advantage of his opponent by using fakes and other techniques to distract, surprise or startle, all in an effort to slow down his opponent's reaction time to his real and hidden attack.

In their book, "The Secrets of Judo," authors Jichi Watanabe and Lindy Abakan (1960), noted that the sensory nerves running through our bodies are excited by external stimuli, and that the resulting excitement is carried to a joint sensory-motor nerve center, in the cerebral cortex of the brain. This joint nerve center then sends out messages to the motor nerve of the cortex, which, in turn, sends messages to the motor nerves in the muscles, causing them to contract. The time it takes for this to happen is called *reaction time*.

Watanabe and Abakan go on to describe at least nine cases in which reaction time is lengthened. Scenarios such as these will be discussed later in this text.

The nervous system processes described above must occur when anyone reacts to external stimuli, regardless of training. However, when approached unexpectedly by an agent, a subject experiences much more than this. Have you ever surprised a friend with a sudden noise or unexpected touch or walked out of a dark room unexpectedly? That friend will "act startled;" jump out of their seat; throw his or her arms up, etc., and look totally surprised. After a few seconds, if not more, your friend will regain his or her composure. Obviously, there is more going on than just a delay in reaction, or sheer "fright."

WITHOUT DEADLY FORCE

Figure 5: The Sensory Motor Nerve Center of the Brain

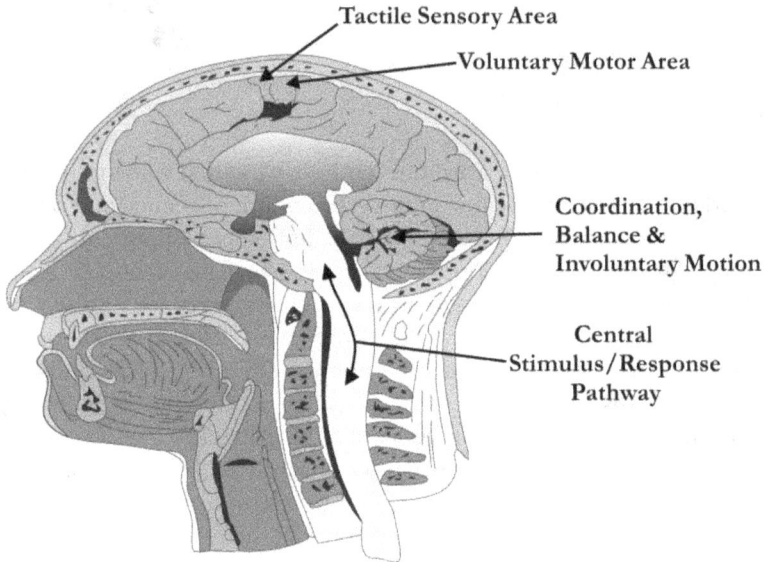

In order for law enforcement officers to gain an understanding of DRT, and what the subject is experiencing when a DRT is initiated, we need to know how our bodies transmit information from our sensory nerves to our brains; how our brains react to incoming information; and how our brains initiate appropriate glandular and muscular responses to the stimuli of interest. In short, we need to know how and why the famous "fight or flight" reaction takes place before the properly approached subject *can figure out which of those two things* to do.

The nervous system runs through all parts of the body (See Figure 6). The chief nerve centers are the brain and the autonomic ganglia. With the onset of a startling event, a subject is able to perceive a touch on his or her body, a change in posture, an alarming sight, or sudden sound because the sensory nerve endings in his or her skin, muscles, eyes and or ears, are excited by the relevant external stimuli. The resulting excitement is carried up from these organs by sensory nerves, through the sensory nerve pathways in the spinal cord, and finally to the sensory region of the cerebral cortex, on the upper surface of the brain. (For a general review of the anatomy and physiology of the human nervous system, see Gardner, 1976. For a review of the relationship between human nervous system and hormonal reactions, see Van Der Graaf and Rheas, 1987. For a review of the function of human sensory systems, and coordinated muscular response in sport or combat, see The Secrets of Judo Watanabe and Abakan, 1960, and Shalif 1988.)

At this point, information about the stimulus becomes available to the interpreting and decision making portion of the brain (the frontal cortex) and a response will be initiated. See Figures 6-9 that follow.

Figure 6: Outline of the Human Nervous System

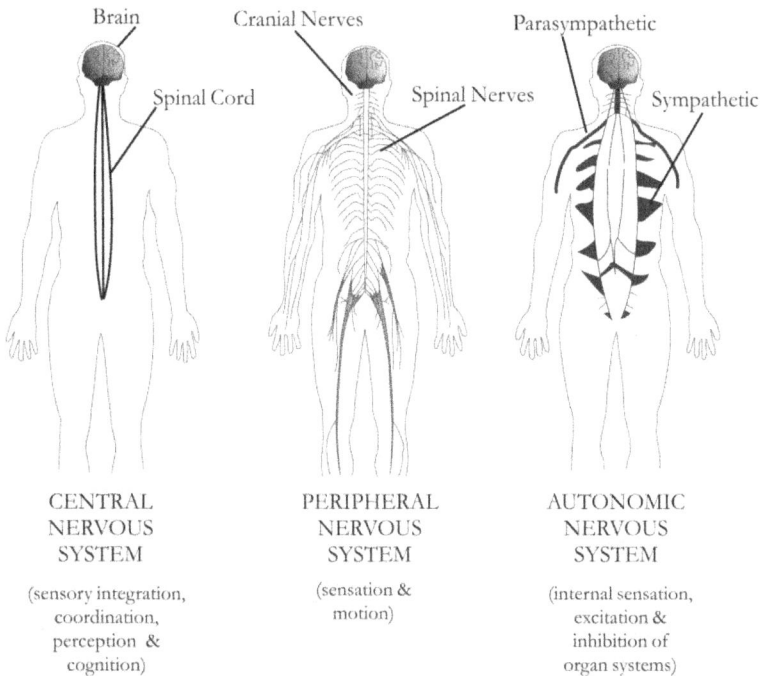

CENTRAL NERVOUS SYSTEM	PERIPHERAL NERVOUS SYSTEM	AUTONOMIC NERVOUS SYSTEM
(sensory integration, coordination, perception & cognition)	(sensation & motion)	(internal sensation, excitation & inhibition of organ systems)

Figure 7: Adrenalin Release Triggered by a Startling Stimulus

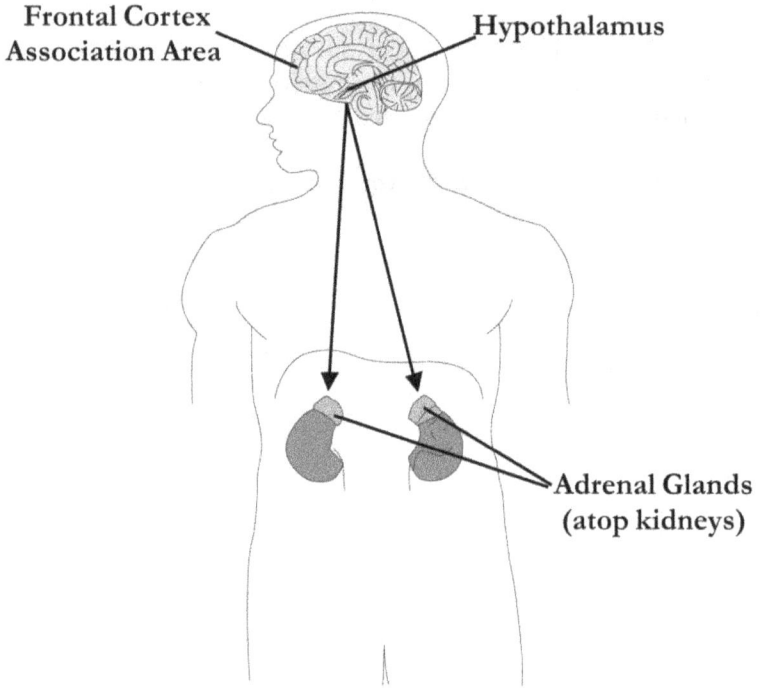

Frontal Cortex Association Area

Hypothalamus

Adrenal Glands (atop kidneys)

Figure 8: Sympathetic Nervous System Stimulation Due to Startle

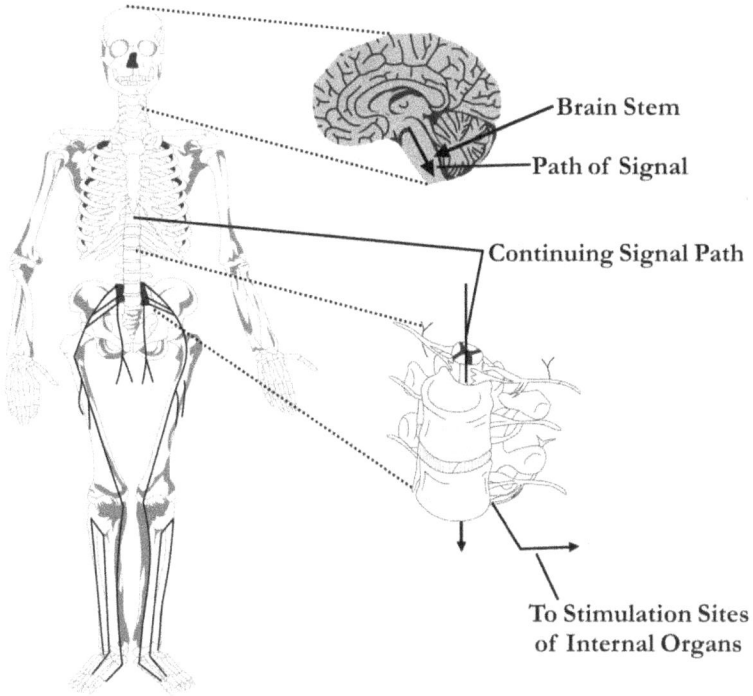

Brain Stem

Path of Signal

Continuing Signal Path

To Stimulation Sites
of Internal Organs

Figure 9: Outline of the Major Motor Nerve Pathways

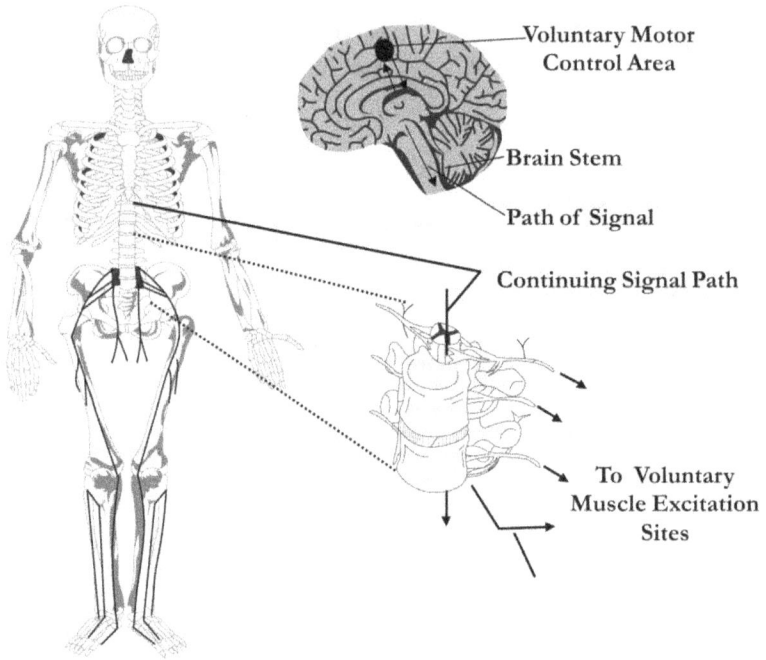

A signal is sent from the frontal cortex to the hypothalamus gland, which is located just under the middle portion of the brain. This gland will trigger the release of the hormone adrenalin by the adrenal glands.

A related signal will be sent down through the stem of the brain to the pathways of the sympathetic nervous system, which controls the excitation of glands and involuntary muscles. The flow of adrenalin from the adrenal glands serves to maintain and enhance these excitatory signals.

A signal will be sent to the motor nerve center which is adjacent to the sensory cortex, then to the motor nerve pathways in the spinal cord, and finally to the motor nerves running minutely to the muscles because the motor nerves cause the proper muscles to contract in a coordinated fashion.

Responses triggered by these signals include:

- A sudden, intense contraction of the major muscles of the body generally causing a forward-ducking, arm-raising startle pattern of sudden movement.

- Dilation of the pupils of the eyes allow for increased visual perception with body hair "standing on end"

- Speedy coagulation of blood from cuts or wounds to prevent and preserve blood loss, chest expansion to increase the volume of air inhaled, lung bronchiole expansion to allow the entry of greater amounts of oxygen

- Contraction of the blood vessels near the surface of the skin causing the subject to turn pale, and further protecting the blood supply from potential wounds, heart and blood vessel dilations to increase the supply of fresh blood to the body

- The release of glucose from the liver into the bloodstream to provide emergency fuel for muscles.

All of these reactions occur before the subject can properly determine what happened, where it happened, and what he or she should do about it. All of these reactions take time.

Even though the major nervous pathways of the body are capable of conducting a large number of signals simultaneously at hundreds of feet per seconds, the cascade of neurological and hormonal responses to such a stimulus are so overwhelming that they can completely paralyze the nervous system of the subject. This paralysis can last for a period of several seconds to a minute or more, provided that the stimulus is truly sudden and surprising. Even if the subject is vaguely aware that danger is present, a startle paralysis of between three and five seconds can often be achieved. Therefore, when a subject is approached unexpectedly by agents (external stimuli), it is an **unalterable fact of physiology** that his or her body requires a certain amount of time to react to those particular stimuli. (For extended discussions of the human startle reaction, its physiological correlates, and of delayed reaction time to startling stimuli, see Cannon, 1939; Landis and Hunt, 1939, Sternbach, 1960; Turpin, 1983; Shalit, 1988; Fernandez and Vila 1989).

While all of the above is useful for classroom teaching and discussion, its real meaning in terms of practical application is that, given the right approach and techniques, the subject of an arrest can be rendered helpless for a few moments. On the other hand, DRT doesn't last forever. In the middle of an arrest I could tell, based on past experience, which phases of this reaction the subject was experiencing. I would try to stay one step ahead of the subject by conceptualizing the stages of DRT that the subject needed to undergo before becoming potentially dangerous or at risk of flight. Look at it like this: "A deliberate action will always be faster than a deliberate response to a deliberate action." A graphic depiction of that conceptualization is presented in Figures 10 and 11.

Figure 10: Stages for a Surprised, Uncontrolled Subject

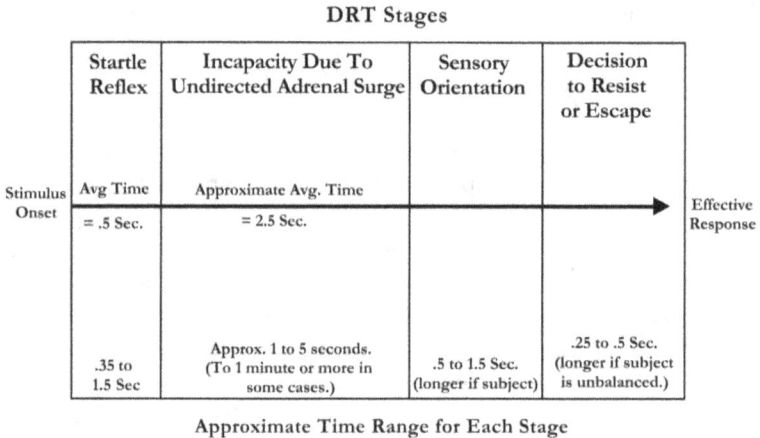

DRT Stages

	Startle Reflex	Incapacity Due To Undirected Adrenal Surge	Sensory Orientation	Decision to Resist or Escape	
Stimulus Onset	Avg Time	Approximate Avg. Time			Effective Response
	= .5 Sec.	= 2.5 Sec.			
	.35 to 1.5 Sec	Approx. 1 to 5 seconds. (To 1 minute or more in some cases.)	.5 to 1.5 Sec. (longer if subject)	.25 to .5 Sec. (longer if subject is unbalanced.)	

Approximate Time Range for Each Stage

Figure 11: Typical DRT Recovery Periods for an Uncontrolled Subject

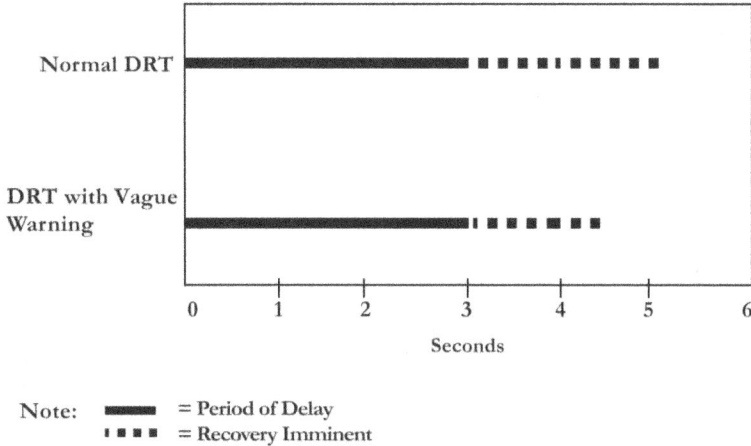

Note: ▬▬▬ = Period of Delay
      ■ ■ ■ ■ = Recovery Imminent

The Traditional Approach in Contrast

In the most well accepted texts designed for police training, there are descriptions of the effects of sudden onset, high stress situations, but these narratives are devoted to the effects of these situations on the law enforcement personnel, and not the subject of an arrest.

In their text, *Street Survival*, Remsburg (1986), Adams, et al (1980), outline arrest methods of the "find cover and challenge, or "stand and deliver" variety but only discuss the use of surprise tactics in the context of an ongoing violent confrontation.

In the text, *The Tactical Edge*, Remsberg (1986) outlines the basic effects of the stress response on a police officer which include a startle response, thought distraction, physical stress, sensory distortion, and lapses of awareness. It is also noted that in situations of sudden stress, these syndromes may cause a police officer to react ineffectively, or to fail to react at all. Much of the rest of the text is devoted to the discussion of methods which can be used to counter the effects of unexpected stress, none of which are effective without thorough training. Remsberg discusses the basics of directional positioning, but only in order to advocate stepping obliquely behind an offender once a violent confrontation has begun, reasoning that this will prevent the subject from using force effectively.

It is ironic that, although both Remsberg and Adams, et al., note the delayed reaction of surprised officers, they never consider the use of initial surprise against offenders. Remsberg, et al., lists methods of seizing the subject, and notes the act of seizure causes a crisis which the subject must resolve by deciding to fight, flee, or obey. The text presents a subject classification from most compliant to most violent and describes a number of increasingly forceful holds which might be necessary to subdue a resisting subject. In the vast majority of the book, *The Tactical Edge*, it is assumed that the subject will violently and effectively resist, an all too likely outcome, given the method of arrest which is proposed.

It is not the purpose of this work to make blanket criticisms of such well known and authoritative references as *Street Survival* or *The Tactical Edge*. Both works present vital information intended for use in training a wide variety of law enforcement officers, and the approach to arrest procedures detailed in those texts reflects the spectrum of sudden and unexpected predicaments in which their readers may find themselves. However, it must be observed that, in planned arrest procedures, or in arrests where coordinated teamwork and stealth can be employed, the use of the DRT system greatly simplifies the problems inherent in the approach and apprehension of the subject of an arrest.

The Innocuous Approach - Considerations

At this juncture, I would like to discuss the techniques involved in inducing and prolonging DRT. This system, unlike others, can be articulated and supported by reference to street experience, and is applicable to the majority of planned street arrests.

As stated previously, DRT's parent process begins with an approach from the circumference (edge) of a circle of subject containment, and with an agent's attempt to shorten the agent-to-subject radius (distance) before the subject detects the agent's actual intentions. I have found that the best approach is one in which the agents attempt to "not blend" in with the surrounding environment. I purposely did not use the word "blend-in" because you don't have to blend in as long as the target is not aware of your intentions. However, in your effort to try and blend-in you will actually make yourself stand out because you are not behaving in a nature manner with the flow of what is taking place around you. You cannot act natural when you intentionally place the undue stress on yourself of trying to blend-in. Therefore, your ability to perform the task is diminished. Second, you are placing mental and physical limitations on what you can and cannot do. It is never a matter of blending in or going unnoticed. All you really want is to have your intensions go unnoticed. This can be accomplished on foot by how you carry yourself as you are moving within the environment where the arrest is going to take place. So, if you act like a cop, you are going to be viewed as a cop from 20 miles away. If you try to blend-in by hiding, people are going to notice that you are trying to hide. In this methodology of making an arrest, you may have to put the cop persona down for a minute. Dressing down or up will help, taking into consideration the ethnic and economic makeup of the area, and by not moving in large numbers; that will help as well. But the key is in your ability to drop one persona and take on a non-threatening one allowing you to approach someone without them discerning your intentions. Remember, on the street, if a guy is wanted, he is always looking out for the unusual; something that's out of place.

One example of looking out of place is something as simple as the way and the length of time you look at someone. Direct "eye contact" for too long is one of the biggest giveaways because it makes you stand out. It is a glitch in the natural ebb and flow governing how people interact in any given society. A casual glance is nothing. However, if eye contact is longer than two seconds or so, the person you are looking at is trying to determine why you are looking at him. His awareness is heightened and he is now scrutinizing you and his surroundings, looking for other signs to confirm his suspicion that something is wrong. Learn how to gather all you need in a quick glance and a friendly smile or hello. Keep it natural. And if you're caught looking too long, nod your head at him, or ask him a question, or make some type of non-threatening comment. We call that, "playing it off."

The DRT inducing approach can also be employed in a vehicle by driving at the same rate of speed as the traffic in the immediate area. Once the subject is located, the driver of the vehicle should not accelerate towards the subject and then come to a sudden screeching stop. The approach should be smooth and gradual, so that the approaching vehicle blends in and does not stand out. The arresting agents must remember that their purpose is to go unnoticed until the moment of attack, using a strategy similar to that of a lion staking an antelope; utilizing stealth to approach to within a specific range (radius) that can be covered before the subject can fully recover from the shock engendered by the sudden attack.

Note: If you are using two or three vehicles, one vehicle can be used to induce DRT as a distraction, while the other two vehicles and personnel are used for the hands-on approach and containment. This is the beauty of the DRT concept. It is flexible and can be used in so many different ways and situations.

THE ELEMENTS OF DYNAMIC CAPTURE

Flaws in the Subject's Perception

There are several specific techniques that will lengthen the subject's reaction time. Consider the angles of approach as illustrated below.

Figure 12: Areas of Central and Peripheral Vision

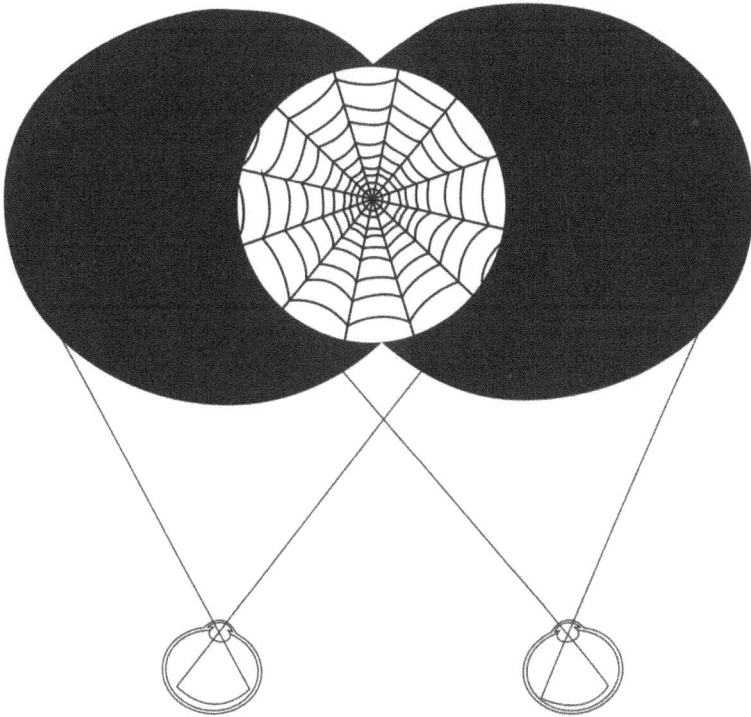

Most people would agree that of the eight angles, the left side, right side, left rear, right rear and the rear, are the best angles of approach. However, the question is why?

Any unimpaired human being is primarily disposed to use visual information to make sense of his or her immediate environment. (For an extended discussion of the structure and function of the human system, see Schiff, 1981.) DRT is engendered in a subject's visual awareness during an indirect advance, because the subject will see the agent's movement obliquely, if at all. Additionally, while the central fovea of the retina of the eye can image an object clearly, the peripheral areas of the retina. This phenomenon is not as reliable during low light or night time activity, because the fovea centralis of the eye needs a great deal of light in order to render this clear image. Therefore, even when an indirectly approaching agent is seen in the subject's periphery, the subject won't receive enough visual information to make an effective appraisal of the situation.

Visual detection of an approach from the side is further impaired because of the placement of the subject's eye. Even at the moment of detection, the subject's "far eye" will be either unfocused, or focused on irrelevant objects in the subject's visual field. This forces the subject to make a head-turn, to properly view and interpret the detected motion. While reorientation occurs, the subject will be unable to identify the approaching agent, or to accurately fix the agent's location in space, until the bridge of the subject's nose is no longer an obstacle for the "far" eye. Only then can both eyes be focused in unison on the agent. See Figure 13.

Figure 13: Visual Orientation to Stimulus Location and "Tip of Nose"

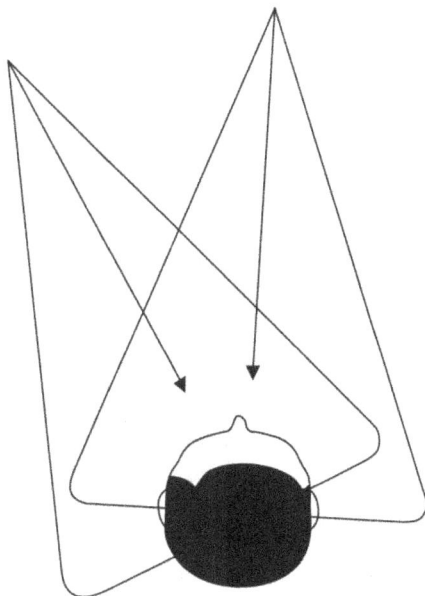

In addition, if the subject can be made to focus his or her attention on a diversionary movement, specifically, one of the agents approaching from an indirect angle in the subject's field of vision, the subject's visual acquisition of another agent approaching at a different indirect angle takes even longer. It would then seem logically advantageous to approach the subject utilizing more than one agent, from multiple, indirect angles.

The above discussion of visual acquisition naturally leads to a consideration of direct approaches from the sides or the rear. Why not always approach the subject from behind, thus disabling the subject's visual system completely; at least for a few moments? Of course, a direct rear approach can be effective, particularly in situations where there is a reasonable amount of environmental noise. However, the approach from any of the indirect angles is usually preferable to direct side or rear approaches. This is because the subject is less likely to effectively hear the advance of the agent.

The human auditory system is able to locate the source of sounds in space by virtue of the placement of the ears on either side of the head. As amazing as it may seem, an unimpaired person can perceive the difference in the arrival times of a given sound to either ear, and can use this information to judge the approximate location of a sound source.

For example, if a sound is made on a subject's left side (left direct approach), the sound waves produced will strike the subject's left ear first, and then the subject's right ear. If the environment noise level is low enough so that the sound can be accurately perceived, even this infinitesimal difference in arrival times will allow the subject to easily locate the sound source to the left, and the subject's visual acquisition of the sound source will begin immediately. Similarly, sounds made as a result of a direct rear approach to a subject will strike the subject from the rear, and will reach both ears simultaneously. The subject can use this information, almost instantly, to locate the sound source.

The flaw in the human auditory location system is the existence of zones of auditory ambiguity which lie on either side of the human head. These zones can be thought of as cones which project outwards at indirect angles from either ear. If a sound is made at any spot on one of these zones, a subject would not be able to distinguish the location of that sound from the possible location of any other sound that could be made in any other part of the zone which lies at the same distance from the subject. See Figure 14.

Figure 14: The Zones of Ambiguity in Human Hearing

As an example, say that an agent, advancing upon a subject from the left rear, accidentally makes a detectable noise. The subject might mistakenly locate the source of the sound as coming from his or her left front or, given the ambiguity of the conditions, the subject might well cast random glances in an attempt to visually locate the source of the sound. Thus, an approach from any of the indirect angles to the subject will usually impair the subject's ability to locate the source of any sounds that are made. This further frustrates any attempt on the part of the subject to properly orient to the presence of an arresting agent, and enhances DRT.

Within the system of DRT, the above mentioned methods of approach are important only because they allow the arrest team to utilize the crucial element of DRT, which is the element of surprise. For example, if the subject is standing half a block away and I shout, "Police don't move!" he or she would probably be surprised, but not very much, and would recover very quickly. If I stood on the opposite side of the street and did the same thing, the subject would again be surprised, but not incapacitated, and again, he or she would recover quickly. However, if I were four to eight feet away from the subject, at an indirect angle, and suddenly and unexpectedly seized the subject as I made my announcement in a clear, stern but conversational tone, it would be a big surprise from which he or she would not quickly recover.

This brings us back to the circular concept of DRT. The subject is the center of that circle. Within the area of that circle is a danger zone. The current prevailing wisdom is that the closer you are to the subject, the more dangerous the subject is (Adams. Et al., 1980; Remsberg, 1986). As stated previously, the implementation of DRT requires thinking in a way which is contrary to that of the older arresting procedures because the system dictates that the further the officer is from the center of the circle at the moment of confrontation or detection, the higher the risk. The subject will have enough time to effectively retaliate before he can be subdued. Conversely, the closer the agent is to the center of the circle at the point of confrontation or detection, the lower the risk to the agent. There is, of course, a distance from the center of the circle where the enforcement becomes ineffective and invites either escape or confrontation.

To further support the effectiveness of closing with the subject in order to induce the effect of DRT, we should consider some of the phenomena that occur when the subject is engaged from a short distance away. Assume that an agent has closed with the subject and initiates the final phase of the arrest process, or that the agent has been detected just prior to his or her decision to seize the subject. In addition to any startle effect that may be achieved, if the agent's movement is first noticed within six to nine feet of the subject, the subject's eyes will automatically refocus, using *binocular depth cues*. This means to use both eyes to tell "near from far" in a way similar to the ears when employed to locate direction. The subject's brain compares differences in the focus of each of the eyes to locate the agent. Although these cues could provide the subject with a more accurate judgment of the position of the agent, this information comes at the cost of an increased time of orienting and focusing his or her eyes. Contrary to popular belief, binocular vision is generally, not useful beyond this range.

At this distance, a large, lateral motion by the agent would require the subject to turn his or her head, refocus his eyes, and reorient his body; while a similar motion at 15 ft. might not require any significant reacquisition time, because of the phenomenon known as motion parallax.

Have you ever watched as a jet airliner slowly traces a path across a clear sky? How easy do you think it would be to watch that same jet airliner if it was only 100 feet away as it passed by you? This is the essence of motion parallax, which occurs because your field of vision expands with distance. When you view an object from a distance, it appears smaller because it occupies a smaller portion of your field of vision than it would if it were closer to you.

Any lateral motion of this object will appear to be slower than it would if the object was nearer to you, because the object will traverse a smaller portion of your visual field than it would at a close range. Often we can compensate for motion parallax by using other familiar objects at the same distance to judge the relative size and speed of the object being watched.

Figure 15: Stimulus Distance, Field of Vision and Motion Parallax

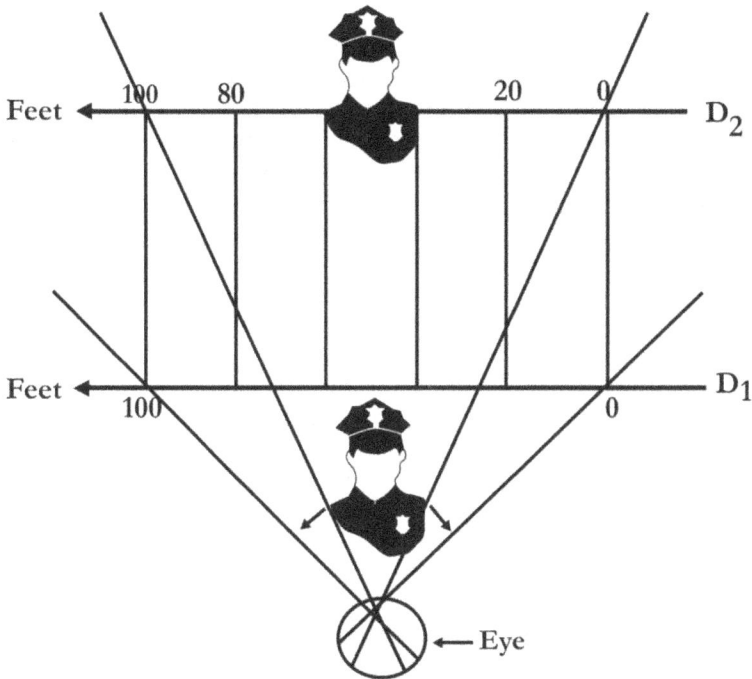

Motion parallax is pervasive in visual perception and is not a phenomenon of great distance, or the motion of uncontrolled objects. To prove this to yourself, completely extend your left arm directly in front of your face, at eye level, and raise your index finger. Next, raise your right index finger to the same level, and hold it directly in front of you, at a distance of about 6 inches away from your face, and align your two fingers. Now close your weak eye, look at your outstretched index fingers, and turn your head, slowly from side to side. If you do this, you will notice that your close finger traverses a much greater part of your field of vision than will your far finger. Now, if you have the patience, open your weak eye and perform the same experiment again. This time, you will not only observe motion parallax, you also experience the same relative difficulty of focusing both eyes on your close finger, which is another important part of the DRT process, described earlier. (For related discussions of motion parallax, see Schiff, 1981)

Case In Point #4: "The Gold Lexus"

Phillip was charged with vehicular homicide in the state of North Carolina. He subsequently fled to avoid prosecution; the act of which is a federal crime. Detectives working the case in North Carolina had reason to believe he fled to New York City. That is how the New York City FBI Fugitive Task Force became involved. My partner was assigned as Case Agent, with responsibility for locating and apprehending Phillip.

Now, I'm not going to explain in detail how tough and skilled the guys are on the Fugitive Task Force squad. We lived each working day and night, literally hunting down the sort of people you wouldn't want to find in your worst nightmares. We sought them in the kinds of places that made hell look like a nice place. Let your imagination tell you what kinds of people could function on a job like that and still remain nice people.

My partner, "G" and I had developed information suggesting that Phillip was possibly staying with an aunt in Queens, New York. We were also able to eventually develop an address for that aunt; she was living in a notoriously tough neighborhood project near the Grand Central Parkway. We conducted several night and day surveillances in the immediate area of the aunt's address and determined two things:

1.   1.   A woman fitting the aunt's description lived in building "C" on the third floor
2.   2.   Phillip did not stay there all the time; he would come and go

We were also able to ascertain information that Phillip had a girlfriend living in Brooklyn off of Eastern Parkway. At some point in the investigation, we were able to develop information that Phillip was going to be at his aunt's apartment on Friday night and he was planning to stay there until around 10:30 pm.

We assembled an arrest team and met around 7:30 pm to recon and stage in preparation of Phillip's pending arrest. We had the physical address for his aunt's building, but did not know which apartment she was staying in and we did not have a search warrant to enter her home.

As such, we decided (the arrest team) would make the arrest as Phillip was leaving the building.

We also had to consider the fact that it was going to be dark outside at the time of the planned arrest. Darkness has advantages and disadvantages. On one hand, darkness made it easier for us to conduct surveillance and get close to Phillip, but on the other hand, darkness was also going to make it more difficult for us to readily identify Phillip.

In addition, we didn't know what time Phillip was going to arrive and there were two methods of egress from the building. That meant we were going to have to set up two teams to cover each exit, but that was the best opportunity we had, so we had to go with it.

That night, all surveillance was conducted from our vehicles. We set up a planned DRT arrest, assuming Phillip would walk toward at least one of the arrest teams. Assignments were handed out. Once the teams were in place, we waited. People were coming and leaving the building all evening long. It started to get late and we became concerned that the information we had was dead. Then, around 11:30 pm, we saw two men leave the building together. One of them appeared to fit Phillip's description, but it was dark out. We were not expecting two individuals. Also, the agents were not certain enough it was him to make a positive ID so we could move on them. By the time they were certain it was him, it was too late! He and his companion had gotten into a Gold Lexus 400, 2-door sports coupe. Darkness was not fully on our side. Because we had no prior intel that Phillip had a car, we were caught a little off guard and were unprepared.

Secondly, we were somewhat surprised given how close the car was parked to the front door of the apartment building, and how quickly they had gotten into the car. Thirdly, we were too far away from the two of them to approach in time to surprise and control them. Also, we were not in position to close-in on the vehicle.

Plan "A" went out the window even before Phillip had closed his car door. It was time for Plan "B". We decided to do a "car stop." To do a car stop on a moving vehicle requires timing and positioning of all the cars involved. When the two of them got in the car, Phillip got into the passenger seat and they pulled out and drove down the street. Our arrest team consisted of five cars, two agents per car. We pulled out behind them. Our plan was to use one car as the tail, positioned at least two cars back. That placed two cars between the subject's car and the tailing agent's car. In that way, we could rotate the tail with a new tail, preventing the subject from realizing he was being followed. We also kept one vehicle in front of the subject's vehicle by having one car ride parallel until the agent was far enough ahead to get in front of the subject's vehicle. It is the responsibility of the car in the first tail position to call everything out and keep all five cars coordinated regarding the location of the subject's vehicle (e.g. street names, intersections, etc.), movement (e.g. moving, left turn, right turn, caught at a "red ball" aka traffic light) and direction (north, south, east, etc.). However, the decision to execute the arrest must come from the Case Agent running the case (my partner).

G was in the car with me and we observed the counter surveillance techniques used by the subject's car. First, he slowed down and everyone behind him had to slow down too. The agent car ahead of the subject's car eventually got too far ahead because the subject's car had slowed down.

Next, the subject's car made a U-turn. He did this to see if anyone else made a U-turn behind him. If someone did, he knew he was being followed. Well, when he made that U-turn, all four agent cars made the U-turn right behind him. G and I knew Phillip now knew it was "On." And, we knew he was heading for the Grand Central Parkway entrance to make his getaway run. The entrance to the parkway was now only two blocks away. If there was going to be a "car stop," the Case Agent had better call it out now or it was going to be a long (or more likely a short) car chase.

For whatever reason, the Case Agent didn't call it and Phillip's car turned onto the Grand Central Parkway. Plan "B" went out the window and we gave chase (Plan C), reaching speeds well over 100 mph. My car was having major problems handling the curves and banks at that speed; whereas the Gold Lexus 400 was built for it. It pulled away from us like we were driving in mud. The car chase was over before it really got started and Plan "C" went out the window as well. We watched the Gold Lexus grow smaller and smaller as it headed toward the Van Wyck Expressway. The car chase was definitely over for us, so we radioed each car to regroup at the first exit off the Van Wyck. It was time for Plan "D" which was to stay in Queens and check out all the known projects in the area to see whether we saw the Gold Lexus 400 again.

Well, we spent about an hour and-a-half going from project to project with zero results. It was about 12:30am, maybe 1:00 am and one of the agents had a brilliant idea (I won't give any names). He said, "Think about this for a minute, what if you just outran the police and left them in the dust? Wouldn't you want to brag and tell somebody about it?" Everybody said, "Yes!" and then he said, "Well, who do guys like bragging to the most after they have accomplished something big?" At the same time, everybody said, "Your girlfriend!"

Plan "E" had just been conceived. All five cars got back on the expressway and we drove from Queens to Brooklyn. His girlfriend lived right off of Eastern Parkway in an apartment on the corner of Kingston Avenue and Eastern Parkway.

Here's the plan: we were sure the Gold Lexus was not Phillips' and we were also sure that the owner of the car was not going to drive all the way to Brooklyn at 2:00am in the morning. That meant Phillip was going to have to take the train. Once we arrived at the apartment, we conducted a quick and easy recon, deciding that the layout was conducive for a DRT arrest. The team identified a subway stop one block away from his girlfriend's apartment. If and when Phillip came out of the subway, there were only two possible routes leading to his girlfriend's apartment. If he walked out of the subway and went straight, that would put him on the quickest and most direct route to her apartment. His other option was to take a right, out of the subway stop, which would have been the longest way to get to his girlfriend's home because it meant walking all the way around the block to get there.

Based on this information, we decided to position the majority of our resources on the shortest path to the girlfriend's apartment. We positioned Car #1 right by the subway stop to get the first visual of Phillip, in case we were right in our assumption. At best, this is deductive reasoning and at worst, it's an educated guess. We now knew what he was wearing so we could ID him right away. We then set up Car #2, parked two-thirds the way down the street, toward the girlfriend's apartment building, on the same side of the street as the apartment building. Car #3 was parked three cars in front of Car #2, on the same side of the street. Car #4 was parked in position to intercept Phillip if he took the long way around the block to his girlfriend's apartment. Car #5 was a roving free safety, ready to respond as backup no matter which way Phillip went.

The plan was for Car #1 to call out on radio when Phillip exited from the subway station. I knew Phillip had to take the shortest path. Why not? Picture Phillip walking down the street, anxious to tell his girlfriend how he outran the cops. He's feeling safe because he's in Brooklyn and the cops who were chasing him, or at least the car he was in, were lost somewhere in Queens. Phillip is thinking life is good and it is going to get even better once he gets to his girlfriend's apartment. He's walking down the block with all of this on his mind. He's on the same side of the street as the subway station and his girlfriend's apartment. He is walking unaware that he is about to enter into a predator vs. prey scenario; completely unaware he is being stalked; that he is the prey this time.

When his approach gets him to about even with Car #2, and just when he is about to pass Car #2, the agents in both Cars #1 and #2 are to exit their cars as rapidly as possible. The agents in Car #2 would use darkness, now the predator's friend, to aid his concealment and intentions. That agent would use indirect angles to close a radius of no more than five or four feet and put "hands on" Phillip as he stood there frozen in the grips of DRT.

The agents in Car #3 would call out all the commands and at least one agent in Car #3 will have a shotgun to cover Phillip, acting as additional stimuli. Cars #1 and #5 are to pull up in their respective vehicles; exit and cover Phillip; establish a perimeter; cover all avenues of escape on that side of the perimeter; make Phillip the center of the predatory circle; add additional stimuli for Phillip to decipher, leading to an inevitable stimulus overload resulting in Phillip's inability to make a coherent or deliberate response.

Well, we sat there for at least an hour and no one showed up. Nothing happened. I was just beginning to think Plan "E" was finished when I heard a crackle over the radio, "Subject is exiting the subway station and headed in your direction."

I was sitting in the passenger seat with my seat reclined all the way back so no one could see me and the other agents in the other cars had done the same, moving into the shadows. I used the side-view mirror to check whether Phillip was coming my way. I didn't see him or anyone else, so I relaxed for a moment, but I kept my head forward and my eyes focused on that side view mirror. Then, I saw movement and appearing in the mirror was Phillip. I kept my eyes focused on the mirror, waiting for Phillip to get even with the car and then for him to move ever so slightly passed the mirror. When I could no longer see him in the mirror, I knew it was time to act! I gave the command, "Execute!" All of the shadows came alive! Phillip never knew what happened! It was almost too easy for us, but that is the beauty of DRT!

THE MOMENT OF CONTACT

Close proximity to the subject at the moment of confrontation also allows the arresting agent to physically unbalance the subject to either the direct-front, left-front, or right-front. Once the subject is off balance, delayed response time is greatly extended. This increase in DRT has both physical and psychological causes.

Psychologically, the firm but fluid seizure of a subject, without excessive violence or pain, will typically confuse the subject, who must now overcome the shock of the sudden contact and construe these actions in order to respond to them. My extensive experience with street arrests has led me to believe that when a subject feels immediate pain, under those circumstances, the "pain cue" will quickly define the sudden contact as an attack. The subject will then actually be enabled to make a timely retaliation, based on the information which the pain provides. In addition, a subject who is suddenly unbalanced is momentarily consumed with the instinctive human aversion to falling. This preoccupation with regaining balance will delay any predicament (Mussen, Conger, Kagan, and Hudson, 1990).

Equally important as the considerations above, in the DRT system, the "preemptive" application of pain to a subject wastes *valuable time*! If the subject has been successfully approached and surprised, the arresting agents or officers should employ only those motions which will directly lead to the control of the subject. Any extra effort in striking or otherwise mauling is, in essence, unnecessary and counterproductive to the true nature of apprehending someone. Why? Because you are "buying time" for the subject to recover from DRT, and to make a direct response to what is now an obvious threat.

Physically, while unbalanced, a subject is incapable of making a forceful response to any perceived threat. As any boxer, wrestler or mixed martial artist knows, all of the rational actions of physical combat require a stable or balanced base from which a direct force can be applied (Watanabe and Abakan, 1960). This is true of both offensive and defensive maneuvers. It is even true of leaping or jumping attacks, where performance necessitates assuming a stable, preparatory stance, then using the leg muscles to "push off" from a floor or other stable platform. In most cases, even hand weapons cannot be effectively employed without a stable base from which to aim or wield them.

In his famous and authoritative book on law enforcement combat tactics and crowd control, Colonel Rex Applegate (1976) wrote:

> "*Physical balance must be retained in the attacker and destroyed in the opponent...A sudden push or pull applied to the shoulders or some other part of the body, will weaken or break the body's balance. Once this is accomplished, an opponent's offensive power and strength, no matter how great, cannot be fully utilized. The man who attacks first and destroys his opponent's balance has a decided advantage, regardless of a difference in size, weight, or physique. Once the opponent is knocked off balance, he should be kept struggling to regain it, and never be allowed to get set.*"

Consequently, I advocate grabbing the subject by the right wrist with your right hand while standing at an indirect angle to the subject (preferably the right side or right rear), and then pulling on the subject's right wrist, extending the arm outward, and thereby upsetting the subject's balance. Once the subject's arm has been extended, the agent should place his or her left hand on the subject's shoulder, redirecting the subject's motion in a circular movement towards the front.

The reasons for these actions are twofold: First, the back of the shoulder is one of the least enervated, and therefore, least sensitive areas of the body, and provides little information about the nature of the contact (Van Der Graaff and Rheas, 1987). Second, by drawing the subject 's dominant arm in the described manner, the agent can quickly and efficiently disturb the alignment of the subject's center of gravity with the stable base formed by the position of the subject's feet (Westbrook and Rattti, 1870).

The stability of any standing object is determined by three factors:
- Weight
- Size at its base
- Position of its center of gravity

Note: See Watanabe and Abakan, 1960

The center of gravity of an object is the "balance point" at the center of the object. The mass of any given portion of the object, on one side of this point, is exactly equal to the mass of the portion which lies in the opposite direction. The center of gravity of a stable, standing object rests squarely over the middle of the base of the object.

If this is true of an object, and the general size, shape and weight of the object remain constant, then the larger the base or bottom support structure of the object, the more stable the object will be. In standing or walking, a human being will unconsciously align his or her body so that its center of gravity will rest directly upon a relatively wide, stable base formed by the position of his or her feet.

Therefore, it would be best for an arresting agent, probably approaching from an indirect, rear angle for all the reasons discussed above to unbalance the subject in a forward direction, perpendicular to an imaginary straight line connecting both of the subject's big toes. Unbalancing the subject in this direction will be relatively easy because pulling the arm will cause the subject's center of gravity to be drawn completely outside of its standing base area. This will leave more than half of the subject's body weight unsupported, at the cost of a movement that is only the length of the subject's feet. If, for example, the arresting agents attempt to unbalance the subject directly to the left or directly to the right, the force and time needed to do so will be increased, because the subject's base will typically be much wider in this dimension. One could imagine a contrived situation where this is not so, such as a subject who has, for some reason, placed one foot directly in front of the other; or who is standing with both feet completely together, but obviously, it is not normally reasonable to wait for a subject to assume such a peculiar stance.

In preparing to use the DRT approach to control and arrest the subject, the agents must bear in mind the size, weight and strength of the subject. The time and effort that is necessary to move a solid object, increases with the mass of the object. Basic principles of momentum and leverage must be used to maximize the effect of the seizure and the unbalance of the subject; particularly when the subject is very large or powerful. The balance of a subject can be most easily redirected when he or she is standing in an unstable posture, or walking at a slow, casual pace and confused about what is happening at that moment in time. Attempting to overcome the inertia of a subject standing in a stable posture, or the forward momentum of a running subject, will require significantly more time and effort, and bring less predictable results.

Proper application of leverage greatly increases the force which an arresting agent can apply to unbalancing a subject. For the optimal leverage, the agent should obtain the wrist and the same-side-shoulder contacts as described above, and fully extend the subject's arm. The agent should then position his or her body so that its full weight can be used to pull the subject off balance, along the line of the subject's outstretched arm. Then redirect the subject in a semicircular, cross-body motion as described above. It may be simpler to pull out and then down toward the ground. However, more times than not, you will get the least amount of resistance when you pull the subject in a semi-circle and then down to the ground.

When the arresting agent uses these tactics, the effect is of using the subject's arm as a "see-saw" lever, with the subject's center of gravity as the balance point. To use this lever to its best effect, the agent must assume a stable stance, which is not as close to the subject that the lever effect is lost, but not so far from the subject that the agent risks losing his or her grip. This position is not hard to find but does vary with the size and shape of the subject.

It often takes a trained martial artist, engaged in a contest, one quarter to one and half seconds to move into a defensive position (Watanabe and Abakan, 1960). However, when the subject of an arrest has been surprised and unbalanced, we maximize the use of the dynamics of DRT, and can easily handcuff the subject when rapid, coordinated and only necessary motions are used.

Once the subject's balance has been broken, the arresting agent should continue to push the subject to the closest rigid obstructing surface, such as the ground, side of a car, or wall. As discussed above, the agent should use only the force necessary to subdue the subject--never more. The subject's muscular contractions can be felt through the arresting agent's hands, so the agent can rapidly determine if more force is required.

Summary

My experience has shown that the streets are getting more and more violent. Criminals are markedly increasing their resistance to arrest, by both attempts to escape apprehension and or by means of violent forms of non-compliance. In my opinion, there is a new kind of criminal out there in urban America; increasingly resentful of legitimate authority and possessed of an attitude forged in a cold and hardened subculture plagued by drugs, gangs, violence and neglect. At the same time, America is becoming a place where automatic weapons in the hands of criminals are commonplace. Is this situation a call for a more violent police force or is it a call for a better trained police force?

When we're operating in this type of environment, do we want to shout, "Police, don't move!" while standing 20 to 25 ft. from the subject; essentially handing him an opportunity to clear his mind and decide whether or not today is a good day to run or retaliate? Or do we want him to give up and go to jail? Do we really want to engage subjects in shoot outs or foot chases that can lead to who knows where? Certainly not as a first choice; and only if necessary! We are too aware that there are other agents in the area seeking to contain the subject, and who are possibly vulnerable to their crossfire. We know too, that the "bad guy" can shoot back. Even if the subject is wounded that doesn't necessarily mean that the subject is unable to return fire. Why burden the subject with the task of making such a decision; one that could risk both our lives?

When a subject has been located on the street, law enforcement officers must employ the advantages of DRT, and must be properly trained in the use of the system. Law enforcement officers should at least be familiar with such concepts as the circle of containment avenues of escape and the expression of the distance between agent and subject as a radius. They must be aware of the methods for penetrating the subject's sphere of awareness without detection.

With training, every law enforcement officer can learn to envision the radius of containment; approach from indirect angles; create a surprising external stimulus to induce a three to five-second startle response in the subject; and properly employ methods to enhance and prolong DRT, taking advantage of the moment of surprise, sensory overload and indecision on the part of the subject.

In addition, all law enforcement officers who are involved in planned arrests should be trained in making reasonable estimates of the time necessary for their arrest team to cover the "radius" distance to the subject. The average time is two to three and half seconds. Such estimates will enable then to construct circles of containment appropriate for particular arrest scenarios, and precisely apply the techniques contained in this book to gain control of the suspect and effect an arrest.

ARREST TEAM TACTICS AND DRT

General Principles

While a single individual can effectively use the techniques of DRT to approach and subdue a subject (ask any experienced mugger), the full effects of DRT are obtained through the efforts of a well-coordinated team. This book will now focus on the proper structure and function of an arrest team for achieving optimally successful arrest dynamics. For any arrest on the street to be successful, each agent in the assigned team must be well schooled in the dynamics of the procedures to be employed, and must also be able to trust in the other members of the team.

Prior to team deployment on the street, the subject must first be positively identified. The location of the arrest must be determined, with consideration given to all possible avenues of escape, and to the utilization of walls or solid objects in order to reduce the potential area of crossfire. At this point, the arrest procedure becomes a matter of teamwork and timing, with all members facilitating an undetected, close approach to the subject. This means your intentions and physical presence are not detected.

Usually, two lead agents are employed. One is designated the immediate "hands on" or "control" agent, while the other agent is the immediate "cover" utilizing a hand gun, causing a distraction, and announcing the presence of the team (FBI!, Police! Don't Move…) and giving orders in a stern, authoritative voice. Within seconds of the first contact with the subject, two or more additional agents should arrive, one covering the subject, and the other assisting with the physical control of the subject. Simultaneously, a perimeter team should be in place to cover for the arresting agents, add to the situational stimuli, cover all possible escape avenues, manage crowd control, and to limit the possible interference of the subject's associates. The perimeter agents will eventually begin to reduce the radius around the subject until all agents are in sight and the subject and agents are in the center and eventually relocated to a designated vehicle.

The reason for the incremental movement of the arrest team is twofold: First, it is easier to initially close the radius with the subject using two individuals as opposed to seven or eight. Secondly, prudent tactics require the strength and safety gained from greater numbers become evident after the initial contact has been made. Third, the introduction of a succession of additional individuals extends, through stimuli and distraction, the effect of DRT on the subject.

Prior to deployment, each agent should be charged with specific tasks that are to be performed during the execution of the arrest. During the arrest, it is critical that agents be acutely aware of their individual areas of responsibility (e.g. securing the left flank, handcuffing subject or covering the arrest team), and how their assignment, and timing of execution fits into the coordinated team effort.

DRT Applications to Arrest Team Tactics
Preliminary Scenarios

These preliminary scenarios are illustrations of the effects of DRT, when applied, misapplied, or initiated by accident, during actual field experience. They should serve to provide a better understanding and feel for DRT's use and how it works. The three scenarios are accompanied by an analysis to provide a "warm up" for the next section, which contains examples for DRT's use in specific situations.

Case In Point #5: "A Practical Problem"

The following is an actual practical problem arrest exercise that I and my squad members performed at the FBI Academy in Quantico, Virginia.

The arrest exercise took place in a practical problem test area called, "Hogan's Alley," which is a mockup town with actual buildings, streets, homes, people, stores, mailboxes, fire hydrants, etc. The agents on my team were given a description of the subject of the arrest exercise: an actor who had been instructed by the exercise coordinators to run from, shoot at, and otherwise physically resist the arresting agents. The subject/actor was armed with a paint gun (pistol).

The information given to the agents about the subject's location was the kind often to be had in real life. The subject worked at a specific hotel, had gone to a particular pharmacy on an errand, and would be returning shortly. The agents knew the subject was armed.

The subject knew of the pending arrest attempt, of course, but had no knowledge of when and where it would be carried out, and was unaware of the agent's locations.

My team of six agents, who I had been working with for some time using the methods involved in DRT, devised a plan to arrest the subject just as he returned to the hotel. They intended to make contact with the subject as he neared the hotel door. In order to do this, an area of containment was created by six agents and an estimated circle and a radius of where we wanted to execute the arrest was created as well.

Figure 16: Hogan's Alley

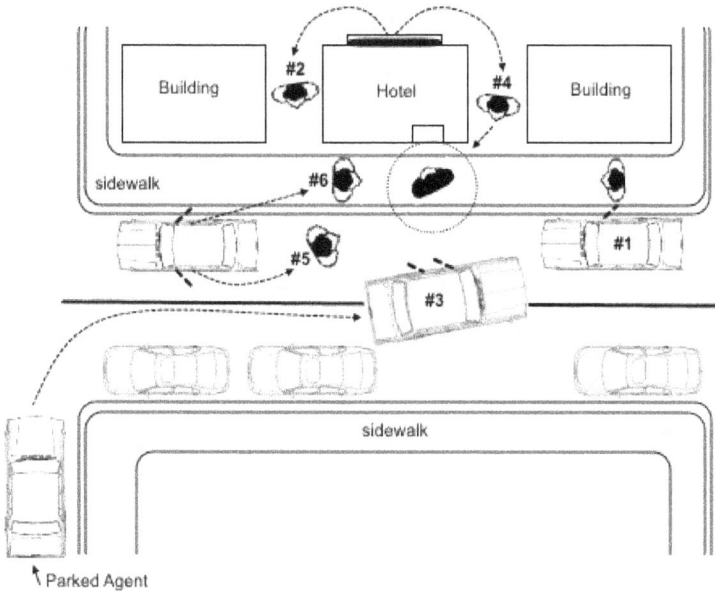

Agent #1 was assigned to spot the subject's approach, to advise the team of his imminent arrival and of his exact description. Agents #5 and #6 were the "hands on" team. Agent #5 was to confront the subject directly, with a verbal challenge. Just before this, Agent #6 was to emerge from the car or the hotel's side door, within the nine foot radius of the circle created by the subject's position at the precise time of the arrest. He was to approach the subject innocuously from an indirect angle. He would first put hands on the subject, in coordination with Agent #5's verbal challenge.

The key was for Agent #6 to move casually but quickly, and to time his approach with that of Agent #5. The objective was for Agent #6 to pass by Agent #5, and to be in close proximity to the subject, on an oblique angle, when the confrontation began. When Agent #5 hailed the subject, distracting the subject's attention, Agent #6 was to turn to the subject, and physically control him as described earlier.

Agent #4's job was to assist Agent #6 in controlling the subject. Agent #4's starting position should align at an indirect angle relative to the position of the subject, which should be a 45 degree angle opposite the angle taken by Agent #4 at a perimeter of 20 feet from the subject; and to time his move off of the movement of Agent #6. Agent #4 was to have his weapon in his hand in a cover fashion but is moving quickly toward the subject, while observing the subject for signs of DRT or the subject's possible, but unlikely, immediate recovery from DRT. This was to be done as Agent #4 is moving, making this determination, while holstering his weapon to assist in handcuffing the subject. The subject should, at that time, be lying face down on the ground or face first against a wall.

Agents # 1, #2, and #3, were assigned to provide cover and to assist if need be. Agent #3 would be the first in line to assist if needed with the control of the subject and then Agent #2 and so on. They were to check for possible associates attempting to interfere with the arrest. Additionally, they would form a semi-circular perimeter, which would also help them to provide crowd control if needed.

The arrest was performed so smoothly that even the team of agents were surprised. Agent #5 informed the subject that he was under arrest, while Agent #6 took hold of the subject's wrist and shoulder. Agent #6 then swung the subject into the nearby wall of the mock hotel building. Agent #6 was able to do this by merely tugging the subject off balance, and then using the subject's own momentum and guiding the subject face first toward the wall. By the time the subject's body touched the wall, Agent #4 was there assisting in controlling and immediately handcuffing the subject. The subject was approached, controlled and handcuffed within three-and-a-half seconds. During the search, a pistol was found tucked into subject's belt, in the front, under his shirt.

This raised a question: why hadn't the subject/actor resisted to the fullest and most drastic extent, despite clear instructions to do so? Upon questioning, the subject/actor stated that he had wanted to and would have pulled his weapon to shoot the agents, but their tactics had left him incapable of making a coherent and deliberate countermove. He said he had been too surprised, and then too "stunned." Between the "surprise" of the challenge by Agent #5, and being led away after cuffing, he had been unable to act.

Subsequent experience in the field has shown this "inability" to be a condition that can be easily and reliably produced if the arrest is well planned and executed with coordination, speed, timing and assigned tasks. This is the essence of DRT and how you can utilize and maximize the phenomena of delayed reaction time.

Case In Point #6: "Standing Still"

This is an illustration of how DRT can accidentally work against the detaining agents. In this case, DRT produced a frustrating delay of response for the agents involved. The two agents were in the field and were interviewing the subject while standing inside a room, close to a doorway. Agent #1 was standing directly in front of the subject, while Agent #2 was standing to the subject's oblique left. There was a door to the subject's right, to the left of both agents.

As the interview began, Agent #1, who was directly in front of the subject, was distracted by a movement to his left. It was merely someone outside the room, walking past the door. At that moment, the subject bolted through the door. Both agents realized what was happening, but given the ambiguous distraction, and the suddenness of the subject's flight, they were momentarily stunned. Yes, trained, experienced and athletic agents were, for a moment, stunned for approximately two seconds at the most, but it was a *delayed two seconds* of inactivity caused by his sudden action of flight. Even worse, Agent #2, who was furthest from the door and less affected (motion parallax) was blocked from giving pursuit, if only for an instant, by the positional proximity of his own partner.

Both agents eventually recovered and were able to follow the subject through the door. In fact, it had not even swung shut by the time they recovered and ran through it. They were unable however, to prevent the subject's flight, even though they had been standing directly in front of them not more than two feet away. In that short period of time, two to two-and-a-half seconds, he had managed to get approximately 60 ft. away from the agents. Fortunately, the subject fell and was captured.

This shows that DRT is not an "unnatural" or strange phenomenon that works only against "bad guys" or people with slow reflexes. Everyone who has been caught "flat-footed" is somewhat familiar with the DRT phenomenon, in a very mild form. The point of the DRT system is to plan and conduct street arrests in a manner that greatly maximizes, even augments, DRT in the subject while minimizing chances of DRT problems for the arresting agents.

Case In Point #7: "Too Far Away To Make It Work"

This is an automobile stop, in which the opportunity to apply DRT was missed. It was a nice Saturday afternoon and based on prior information, agents were conducting a three-car surveillance in the area of a low income housing project in Brooklyn. We were trying to locate a subject wanted for murder whose name was Zebadiah. We will call him "Z" for short. Z was a young guy in his early twenties, about six feet tall and weighed about 160 pounds. We had been searching the area for about an hour and then the lead car spotted Z. He was standing on the walkway in front of an apartment building about 50 ft. from the curb and about 20 ft. from the door of the apartment building.

Now, if Z had been standing on the sidewalk near the curb, the most effective DRT method for arresting him would have been for the two cars of agents to "frame" the subject. This would have entailed the lead car reporting to the second car, upon spotting the subject. The lead car would then have driven up in a causal manner, just beyond the subject, coming to a quick halt as close to the subject as possible. The second car would drive up to the subject at the same time, halting just before the subject. This coordinated action would have "squeezed" the subject between two suddenly arriving vehicles. Such an approach has two beneficial effects: 1) a quickly created area of containment; and 2) the delay of coherent reaction (DRT) produced in the subject.

However, in this case, Z was not standing near the curb; he was 50 ft. from the curb. The ideal DRT method in this case would have been to park the vehicles far enough down the street to be unnoticed but close enough so that at least one of the cars had a visual on Z or one of the agents who was going to approach Z.

Note: A distance of 50 ft. is too much distance to cover by a group of agents without them being detected and the distance is also too great to use vehicles as a means of approach as well because you still have to deal with the lack of containment. Vehicles will only get you within 50 feet of Z. This creates a radius of 50 feet, which cannot be covered in less than two-and-a-half seconds, which is the extent of Z's DRT.

Therefore, we had to slow it down; drop off two "hands-on" dressed down agents who could walk undetected in the area. The two agents would walk down the sidewalk, toward the targeted building, in radio or cell phone contact with the agents in the two vehicles located down the street. Once, the two agents spot Z, they would turn right, off the sidewalk, and head onto the walkway leading up to the building and to Z. Once the two agents turned onto the walkway heading toward Z, the vehicles down the street would start to drive toward the front of the target building, trying to time their arrival to just a moment after the two agents make physical contact with the subject. The arriving vehicles should, at this point, arrive with a sudden stop; all of them should jump out of their vehicles shouting, "FBI" or "Police. Don't move!", thus adding additional stimulus overload to Z, covering him, setting up a perimeter, cutting off all avenues of escape, crowd control and assistance with the control and extraction of Z. Well, the arrest didn't actually go as we planned it.

What actually happened was, the lead car spotted Z without informing the second car. Furthermore, the lead car passed the subject by a significant distance before halting. The lead car ended up stopping approximately 19 ft. pass the point on the curb which would have placed the car perpendicular to Z's exact physical location. Now, add on the fact that Z was standing approximately 50 feet from the curb, which now placed him 70 ft. or so from the arrest team. The team was now in an awful position to effectively execute the arrest.

The agents in the lead car jumped out of the car and ran toward Z shouting FBI, police, etc. At this point, the agents in the second car observed a typical DRT response in Z, but the delay reaction time produced in Z, that could have been used had we been closer, was lost. Z had the time to pull himself out of shock and surprise at seeing the agents running directly at him, shouting. By the time they had closed a quarter of the distance, Z's surprised look began to fade. One telltale sign is the eyes, when a person is surprised, their eyes get big and they get locked onto whatever it was that surprised them, but when you start to see the eyes move and dart around, that tells you the subject is deliberately evaluating his options and trying to come to a decision. So, when the agents emerged from their vehicles, raced toward him, and ordered him to submit to being apprehended, he made an organized decision to make a break for it. He ran for the door of the building directly behind him.

One agent from the second car was acutely aware of how DRT worked and realized the moment the first car stopped that they would not get to Z before he could recover and was able to run, so he had gone around the rear of the second car, in order to salvage the faulty area of containment and tactics. It was that agent who first ran in pursuit of Z. Z reached the project building door successfully, but he found it was locked. He was able to sense the movement of the group of agents in pursuit and tried to evade to his right and was successfully running away until the agent from the second car, who anticipated what way Z would run, caught up with him and tackled him.

It would seem that a resourceful agent and a locked door were the most fortunate aspects of this scenario, but there was one more fortunate thing to occur: the search showed that Z had been armed, but decided to only run.

Analysis

The events in this arrest show the necessity of carefully considering containment first, with an eye toward taking advantage of the momentary DRT benefit upon approach. The less than optimal positioning resulted in the subject's having the time to recover from the DRT phenomenon; rally enough to make a non-compliant decision, and act on it. His sudden actions seem to have had the DRT effect on the arresting agents, who were not completely into position. The agents accidently wound up in the reactive posture they had needed to produce in the subject. He should have been reacting to what they did, not the other way around. As a result, not only was the success of the arrest endangered, but the agent's safety was left to chance and more force was used than would have been otherwise necessary.

Consider the manifestations of DRT in this scenario. A DRT reaction will take place whenever the actions performed are swift and surprising. It will only benefit the arrest team if:

- Containment is provided effectively and is an essential part of the arrest plan.
- The "hands on" agents are close enough to the subject, within a two to two-and-a-half second radius at the beginning of DRT to immediately execute the arrest.
- The agents follow through with assigned actions in a thorough, coordinated and timely manner.

This prevents delays in the action that could allow the subject to recover and possibly initiate a DRT response in the agents, by making a sudden move to escape.

DRT APPLICATION TO ARREST TEAM TACTICS EXAMPLES

Example 1 – Two Vehicles, Single Subject

The illustration below depicts a two vehicle, drive-up arrest. The subject may be on the sidewalk, exiting/entering a building or exiting/entering a car. In such a situation, a vehicular approach is made, in both speed and manner, to resemble the "coincidental" drop off of a passenger at the subject's location. Vehicle #1 contains a minimum of two agents, and is the lead vehicle whose driver sets the pace of the approach. The driver of Vehicle #2 should immediately follow Vehicle #1, but should63 not tailgate Vehicle #1.

Figure 17: Two Vehicles, Single Subject

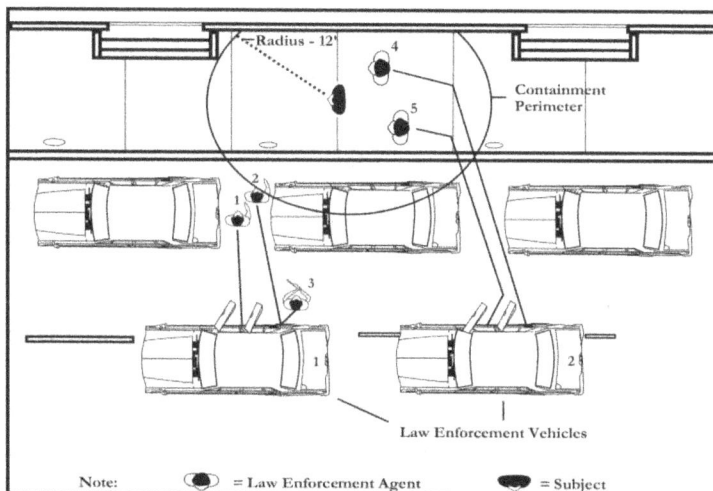

Figure 17: Two Vehicles, Single Subject

When the two vehicles come to a stop, they should be as close to the sidewalk as possible. If there are cars parked on the street, the drivers should ensure there is enough room to open the doors of their vehicles quickly and completely; enabling all of the agents to make a rapid exit from the vehicle. In addition, it is of paramount importance that the drivers pull up to the curb so that the subject is, at first, not sure about what is actually going on and so that the subject is framed by the two vehicles as they come to a stop. If the approach to the subject is successfully performed in this way, it will enable part of the arrest team to quickly cover the distance to the subject and for the other part of the team to cover the subject's flanks while the pre-assigned "hands on" agents are effecting the actual seizure of the subject.

In the example given here, Vehicle #2 contains the two "hands on" agents. Although Vehicle #1 arrives first and is acting as a distraction, the agents in Vehicle #2 must determine the best moment and angle to close with the subject, and the agents in Vehicle #1 must wait and time their exit with that of the agents in Vehicle #2. The agents in Vehicle 1 must wait for both the agents in Vehicle #2 to exit their vehicle and then move as those agents make their final approach to the subject.

While the vehicle approach is slow, the agents exiting from the two vehicles must be fast and swift. The two "hands on" agents must utilize indirect angles to reach the subject before the other agents move within close quarters. The subject will first attempt to attend to these two agents, but then be distracted by the approach of the agents from Vehicle #1. The primary responsibilities of the agents from Vehicle #1 are to cover the subject, distract the subject, and to cut off any avenues of escape on the subject's rear flank. At least one member of this "cover" team should have some type of shoulder weapon. One member of this cover, at the right moment, moves from the cover team assignment to assist in the control and handcuffing of the subject.

The arrest team being thus deployed, the subject will be startled by the sudden approach of the agents. He or she will attempt to attend to the primary startle stimulus presented by the "hands on" team from vehicle #2. The subject may consider an escape in the opposite direction from these agents, but will realize that this escape route has been blocked. As the subject attempts to redirect his or her attention to the primary stimulus, a "hands on" agent will close-in and seize the subject, forcing subject to the ground while giving orders to the subject. While the cover agents point their weapons at the subject, the other "hands on agent", obscured by the method of approach, will assist in the capture and apply handcuffs to the subject.

From the time the agents exit the two vehicles, to the completion of the procedure, the entire execution of this arrest should require no more than seven seconds.

Example 2 – Four Vehicles, Subject with Associates

In this second illustration, a source has identified the subject and a description of the subject has been relayed to the vehicles involved in the arrest. The arrest team consists of three vehicles each containing two agents; a van containing one driver; one agent in the passenger seat and four agents secreted in the back of the van.

Figure 18: Four Vehicles, Subject with Associates

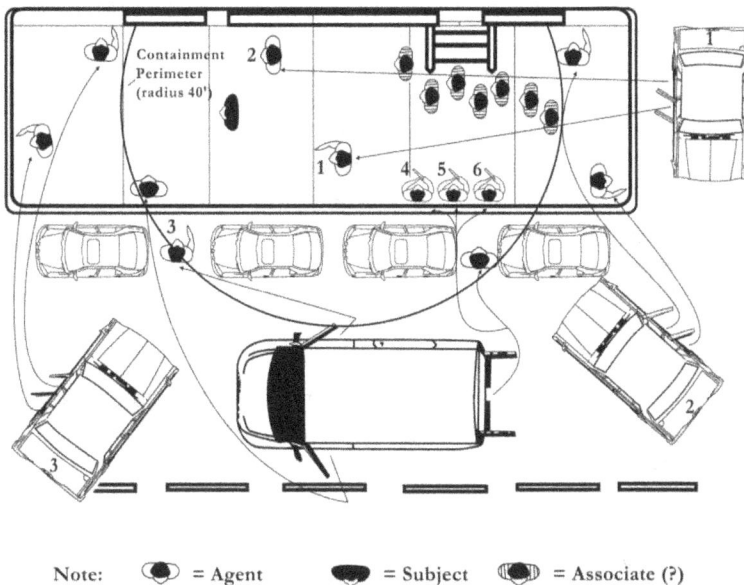

Note: ● = Agent   ● = Subject   ● = Associate (?)

All four of the agents in the back of the van should wear raid jackets and have shoulder weapons. Their assignment is to cover anyone near the subject, and to secure the immediate perimeter around the subject. The drivers and passengers in the other vehicles should be dressed down agents who can flow well with the environment where the arrest is taking place.

It is the task of the agent in the passenger seat of the van to keep visual contact with the subject, and to react to signals from the lead agent on the arrest team. He or she will direct the agents in the rear of the van to initiate the arrest, and will advise the agents in Vehicles #2 and #3 via radio that the arrest has begun. The agent in the passenger seat of the van will then exit the van and advance, with weapon drawn, so as to cover the subject in close proximity.

Upon receipt of the signal to begin the arrest, the driver of the van will exit the van via the driver's side door, then move around to the front of the van and continue on towards the subject, with his or her weapon drawn. If the arrest has been properly executed to this point, the van driver will then holster his or her weapon, and assist in the handcuffing of the subject.

The assignment of the agents in Vehicle #2 and #3 is to secure the flanks of the subject, and to establish an outer perimeter which will serve as a last barrier against a possible escape attempt. These vehicles should be placed approximately one to two blocks away from the immediate area of the arrest, so that the subject will not be alerted by their presence. Vehicle #2 and #3 can move into their assigned position a few seconds after the deployment of the arrest team and the immediate perimeter team, as mentioned above. It is easier to conceal a large arrest in a hostile environment by moving the team in sequential increments.

As background for this arrest scenario, consider this subject to be armed, extremely dangerous, and to be traveling with two associates. Assume that the source has advised the subject is standing in front of a specific building, and there are at least five other individuals standing outside the building.

As stated before, Vehicle #1 contains the two primary arresting agents. Agent #2, from Vehicle #1, is the DRT trained "hands-on" agent and will have a handgun but will not remove it from the holster, because both of the agent's hands must be free in order to surprise and control the subject, and to direct the subject toward the ground. Agent #1, from Vehicle #1, will have one hand on a handgun concealed by the agent's coat or other similar article of clothing, and will approach the subject in support of the movements of Agent #2.

When Agent #2 reaches for the subject, Agent #1 should draw the concealed weapon and cover the subject, which is the immediate threat. In this case, Agent #2 will begin the process of handcuffing the subject with the assistance of the driver of the van. The agent that occupied the passenger seat of the van will then assist Agent #1 in covering the subject. If any additional help is required to handcuff the subject, Agent #1 will also assist, while the passenger of the van continues to cover the subject.

Given the assignment for all of the agents in this scenario, as they have been outlined above, the necessary timing of the execution of these assignments can now be addressed. Prior to any other activity, the agents in Vehicle #1 will "square the corners," which means to drive around the block to obtain a visual contact with the subject; confirm the subject's location and description; and relay this information to the rest of the team. The agents in Vehicle #1 will then advise the driver of the van to move the van from a preliminary location, usually a block or so away, to a "double parked" position in close proximity to the subject, and on the same side of the street where the subject is located. The agent in the passenger seat of the van should have a visual contact with the subject, and should be able to observe the approach of the two agents from Vehicle #1.

With the onset of the arrest, Agent #2, from Vehicle #1, will approach the subject with Agent #1, in support. As Agent #2 is about to reach out for the subject, the agent in the passenger seat of the van should make a sudden and dynamic exit from the van. This distracting movement will add to the subject's state of confusion and will prolong the subject's delayed reaction time. The subject should then be placed on the ground and handcuffed before there is any chance of recovery. The agents in the back of the van, having been signaled by the van passenger's sudden exit, will immediately exit the rear of the van and will proceed to cover and control any possible associates of the subject. Finally, the agent in Vehicles #2 and #3 will deploy, flanking the subject and establishing the outer perimeter, as specified above. Once the subject has been secured and perimeters established, the teams will return to their vehicles in the same order in which they deployed, with the perimeter team loading up last. Once everyone is back in their assigned vehicles, the team departs together in the same order in which they arrived.

Example #3 - Vehicular DRT, Two Vehicles, Single Subject

Although the below diagram illustrates an arrest utilizing two vehicles and four agents, the principles of approach to the subject are essentially the same as those of the previous example. Again, the object of the team is to get as close to the subject as possible before the subject becomes aware of the agents and their intentions. As in all of the previous illustrations, it is important that the subject be made the center of a circle of containment, which means, in this case, that the two vehicles must be positioned so that the subject is framed between them. The strategic difference between this scenario and those discussed earlier is that the vehicles are actually used to engender the startle effect in the final stage of the arrest. It is critical therefore that both of the vehicles come to a stop in very close proximity to the subject, but not so close that the subject is in real danger of being struck by either of the vehicles.

Figure 19: Vehicular DRT, Two Vehicles, Single Subject

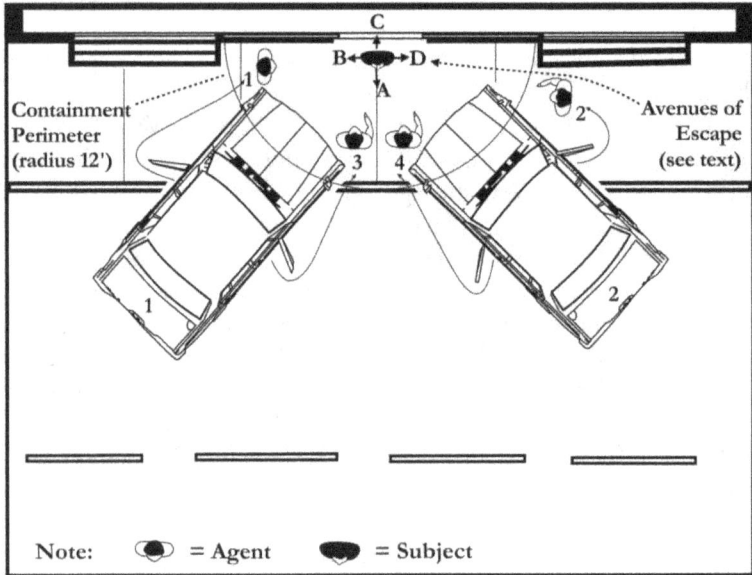

As both vehicles draw close to the subject and stop, the agents in the front passenger seats of the vehicles will make rapid exits with weapons drawn. These agents will proceed to secure the flanks of the subject, and to prevent a possible rear escape into the building. During this sudden advance, the two agents must be careful to coordinate their movements so that each is fully aware of the other's position. In particular, they should be careful not to form a linear alignment with the subject in the middle. That type of "agent-subject-agent" formation would expose each agent to crossfire from the other agent. Once again, an approach from indirect angles is preferable to direct approaches.

In all of the previous examples, physical contact was immediately made with the subject. In the current example however, Agents #1 and #2 will maintain a distance of approximately five to six feet, utilizing available cover. The agents in the driver's seats of Vehicles #1 & #2 will exit their vehicles as rapidly as possible, with weapons drawn.

Agents #3 and #4 will now rapidly exit the vehicles and approach the subject as shown, securing the possible escape avenues, which are marked "A" and "B". The Agents will loudly order the subject to stand still and to put his hands "in the air."

A sudden and successful deployment in the pattern described here will result in a "*full blown*" DRT effect. This will induce a clearly recognizable startle reaction by the subject, and a reflexive focus of the subject's attention on the closest and most readily identifiable threat. Thus, as the execution of the arrest is initiated, the subject in this scenario will, in all probability have assumed the typical ducking posture of the startle pattern, and will have both eyes focused on the front grill of the agent's vehicle. Once it is clear to the arresting agents that the subject is indeed experiencing DRT, has no objects in his hands, and is compliant with shouted orders, one of the primary arresting agents (Agent #1 or #2 previously assigned as "hands-on"), will holster his or her weapon, and move quickly towards the subject from a rear indirect angle. This agent should not move towards the subject directly from the rear because this approach would bring the agent into the linear line of fire.

Once the "hands on" agent has made physical contact with the subject, the agent should immediately order the subject to comply, unbalance the subject to the ground or a wall and begin to handcuff the subject. When the other primary arresting agent (who is on the subject's opposite flank) has observed that physical contact has been made, that agent should move in with weapon holstered, and assist in the physical control of the subject. Agents #3 and #4 will continue to cover the subject; to maintain the immediate perimeter; and to ensure the safety of the primary agents.

Example 4: One Vehicle, Deployed Agent, Single Subject

In this next illustration, we assume that surveillance has confirmed the subject's identification, and has advised the arrest team that the subject was in the Eastern portion of the South side of the street. We also assume the subject has been properly identified, that a description has been given to the arrest team, and the team has been informed that the subject is walking in a certain direction, possibly towards a specific destination, such as a place of work or a train station. Armed with this information, the arrest team will lay in wait at an intercepting point further along the subject's known path.

Figure 20: One Vehicle, Deployed Agent, Single Subject

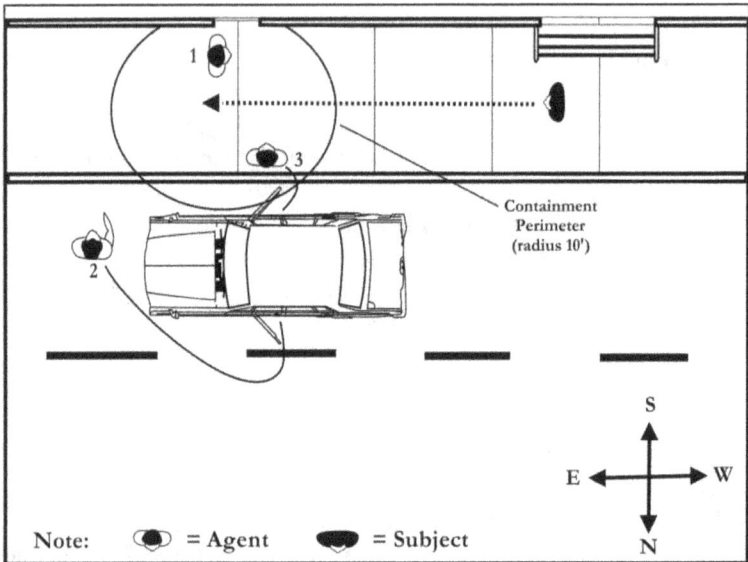

First, a back-up vehicle, containing a minimum of two agents will be positioned at a point where the subject will pass. If at all possible, the vehicle will be parked by the sidewalk. If this is not possible, the vehicle will be doubled parked. The agents in the vehicle should use the radio to regularly (but not incessantly) update the rest of the arrest team on changes in the subject's position. An agent trained in DRT (Agent #1) should stand on the street near a building by the vehicle, possibly in a recessed doorway. The agent in the vehicle should signal the agent on the street when the subject is approaching.

Once the agent on the street (Agent #1) has made visual contact with the subject, he or she should continue to wait until the subject has taken at least a half step past the agent's position before moving in to seize the subject. Allowing the subject to pass affords the "hands-on" agent with the best window of opportunity to induce DRT, through an approach to the subject's right rear. In order to physically control the subject, the agent should then perform a sudden, fluid seizure of the subject's right wrist, with the agent's right hand, immediately followed by an unbalancing pull outward (or forward), but at all times pulling so that the arm is outstretched and away from the subject's body; then applying downward pressure to the subject's right shoulder with the agent's left hand. If it is known that the subject is left hand dominant, a characteristic shared by roughly ten percent of the general population, this procedure should be performed from the subject's left rear, grasping the subject's left wrist with the agent's left hand, etc.

Having grasped the subject in this manner, the agent should now physically redirect the subject through a left to right cross-body swing of the agent's arms combined with left to right twist of the agent's torso, using only the amount of force which is necessary to deflect the subject from his or her original path. Of course, this would be a right to left redirection in the case of a subject known to be left handed. While performing this action, the agent should announce who he is and order the subject to comply in plainly audible, stern but conversational tones, and should be careful to step *with* the subject as he or she is being redirected to a wall or to the ground, because it is possible to lose control of the subject by swinging through too great an arc.

The two agents in the vehicle should anticipate the advance of Agent #1, and begin their rapid exit from the vehicle just before Agent #1 makes physical contact with the subject. Agent #3 will immediately assist Agent #1, while Agent #4 will maintain his or her distance and cover the subject.

Two Agent Arrest Tactics

In each of scenarios above, the success of the arrest procedure is dependent upon the use of tactics which cause subject DRT; which maximize DRT in the arrest process; and which optimize the efficiency of the arrest team during the period of DRT. A safe and effective arrest can be made when all of the participants are thoroughly aware of their respective assignments, and of the critical interdependence of their roles in the arrest procedure.

Methods of approach that can be used by two agents are illustrated Examples A, B and C. All of these methods can be used on a busy street sidewalk or when the subject is standing alone. These methods are for use when a backup team is, for whatever reason, unavailable.

Figure 21: Two Agent Arrest Tactics

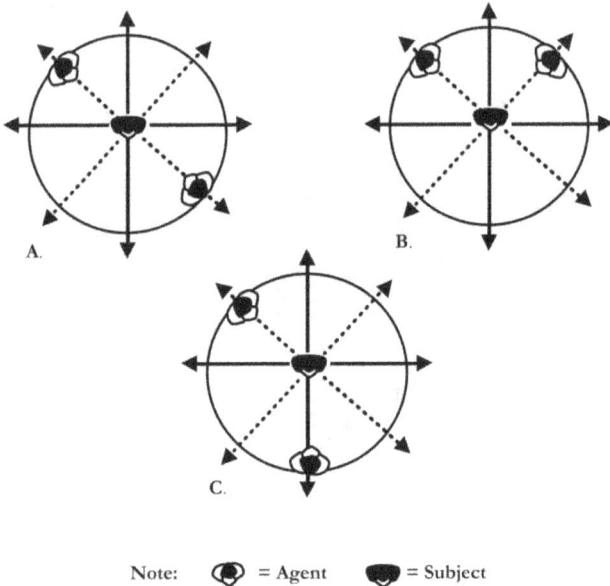

Note: ⊕ = Agent ⬤ = Subject

Example A: Division of Attention

In this example, the agents approach the subject indirectly, but from opposite sides, so that the subject cannot focus attention on both agents simultaneously. The agent approaching from the rear should be the primary, "hands-on" agent in this situation, but this does not necessarily mean he or she must be the first agent to make contact with the subject. Once the initial contact is made, the agents should proceed to subdue the subject along the lines discussed above.

Example B: Reliance upon Stealth

In this example, the techniques and assignments used are the same as those employed in Example A. An initial examination of this diagram might lead to the conclusion that the subject has several open avenues of escape. Agents who use DRT properly, however, can make use of the visual and auditory ambiguities produced by correct angles of approach, reach close proximity as they begin the arrest and take advantage of the subject's inability to attend to both of them simultaneously. Such actions will close the apparent routes to freedom, and allow the agents to subdue the subject before a timely response to their advance can be made.

Example C: The Use of Diversion

Example C is different from both Examples A and B in that one of the agents employs a deliberate distraction. It could be soliciting some mundane piece of information from the subject, such as the correct time, or the directions to a well-known location. Of course, as the subject is distracted, the other agent would approach from the rear of the subject, opposite the side on which the first agent presented the diversion, and the team would then use the DRT tactics discussed previously to make the arrest.

Case In Point #8: "The Trickster"

Moses was a guy I had introduced in a Case In Point in my first book, "*C.A.R.E. An Investigative Way of Life*," I explained that he was wanted for a murder he was alleged to have committed in Los Angeles, California. In my first meeting with Moses, believe it or not, he managed to make me look like a complete idiot by leading me to believe he was not the person we were there to arrest and that the person I was looking for would be arriving that evening on a greyhound bus. This he did even though I had a photograph of Moses and he was standing right in front of me, and I had six trained and heavily armed agents standing right there with me. I basically told them, "He's the wrong guy…let's go." So, based on the information Moses the trickster gave me, and of course, my gullibility and corruptible interviewing skills at the time, I had my arrest team leave that location (and the suspected murderer) and we eventually drove to the New York City Port Authority Bus Terminal waiting for a person who did not exist, while the real suspected murderer laughed his way out of town.

Well, as I said in the first book, the story didn't end there and it doesn't really end here either because in this particular Case In Point, I'm going to tell you how we eventually came to see Moses again. However, how he ended up coming back to New York City is another story for another book.

Again, it was a beautiful day for an arrest. The sun was shining brightly above in all its glory and majesty and all the flowers, grass and trees were bathing in it. We had information that the infamous Moses, the trickster and suspected murderer, was supposed to arrive at 1:30 pm, at a bus stop in Long Island, New York, just outside Queens, New York. The arrest team staged approximately three or four blocks away from the bus stop. It was a direct route from our staging location to the arrest location. We came up with the following game plan:

We knew where and when the bus would arrive. We also knew where the bus would drop off its passengers. We were also familiar with the entire physical layout of the bus station as well as the surrounding area. We knew because we went out there twice to observe how the buses came in and dropped off passengers, and how the people waiting to pick up passengers would congregate any time a bus was about to pull into the station/bus stop. We also observed and noted how some people pulled up in their cars and waited. We watched the dispersal patterns of the people as they disembarked from the bus. We needed to be as familiar as possible with what went on at the bus station. This gave us an advantage over the trickster and would allow us to maximize the advantages of DRT.

We knew he was planning on meeting someone when he got off the bus. The person he was planning to meet was actually our informant in the case. We didn't know the exact order in which the passengers would disembark from the bus; Moses could get off first or be the twenty-first to disembark.

We knew there would be a lot of people at the bus stop waiting to pick up passengers. We would put two dressed down agents in the crowd of people who were waiting to pick up passengers. Agent #1 would be the "hands-on" agent and Agent #2 would be the immediate "cover agent." They were expected to blend in with the crowd and go unnoticed. Next, we positioned two spotters, away from the immediate area of the bus and the crowd of people waiting for the bus to arrive. But, we placed them in positions where they had a good view of the bus from different vantage points. Their responsibility was to spot the subject coming off the bus and relay that information, along with a detailed description of what the subject was wearing; his position in relationship to the arresting team; whether he was alone; and what he was doing. Was he walking or looking around? Is he acting suspicious? Is he looking directly at one of the agents? What direction was he walking in, etc.? We do this because we don't want the agents who are standing at the bus door scrutinizing everyone who is coming off the bus. If the subject is on the bus, he knows he is wanted by the law for murder so he is definitely not going to get off the bus first. No, he is going to hold back, looking out the bus window for something that looks out of place. He wants to make sure it's safe before he gets off that bus! So, we use a spotter who is positioned too far away for him to notice.

Next, we assigned two flanking agents, Agents #3 and #4. Their responsibilities are to act as another distraction (stimuli); set up an inner perimeter; cover Agents #1 and #2; and cut off all avenues of escape on the right and left flanks. The remaining agents should remain outside the main group of people who were waiting for the bus to arrive. Their main responsibility was to set up outer perimeters with a radius of no more than 15 to 20 ft.; cover and cut off all avenues of escape, and crowd control.

Note: There are essentially four coordinated, interlocking groups working within the arrest team.

1. Spotters
2. Hand-on & immediate cover person
3. Inner perimeter – cover and containment persons
4. Outer perimeter – cover and containment (wearing raid jackets, "FBI") persons

It was approximately 10:00 am and once everyone's assignment had been given, it was time to drive over to the bus stop. We didn't want to miss the opportunity to get the best parking spaces for the incoming 1:30 pm bus from Miami, Florida. We also wanted to do one more recon to make sure we didn't miss anything. After determining we had not missed anything, it was time for everyone to take up their positions.

Because the trickster and I had met four months ago, when he tricked me like I was a rookie, I didn't want to take the chance of him seeing me and remembering my face. Therefore, I stayed in the background helping to coordinate the arrest. Around 12:30 pm, people started showing up, driving into the parking lot. Some of them stayed in their cars, others got out of the car, some to smoke a cigarette, others to stretch their legs and walk around. Some of them took a seat on the nearby park benches, put in place just for that purpose. Agents #1 and #2 blended in so well it was hard for me to spot them and the inner perimeter team. As the time slowly approached 1:25 pm, we saw the bus approaching. The bus came to a stop right where we expected. The bus's passengers started disembarking and more than half of them had gotten off the bus and we had yet to see the trickster. I couldn't help but think to myself, "not again." Then, over the radio I heard the spotter say, "We have a confirmed visual on the subject. He's about to step down the steps of the bus."

Agent's #3 and #4 move into flanking position before the subject can get off the bus. By staying close to the bus and using it to hide their presence, they go undetected. Agent #2 is moving within the crowd of people (who are looking for family members, friends and associates), but is moving directly toward the center of the subject's vision...still undetected. Because he is not making eye contact with the subject, he even appears to be totally oblivious to the subject's presence. Agent #1 moves into position from what will be an indirect angle on the subject's rear right, coordinating his movement with that of Agent #2.

Agents #5, #6, #7 and #8 are moving discreetly as well to set up the outer perimeter; all the while gauging their movement, pace and approach based on Agents #3 and #4. All of the agents were aligning themselves according to and in anticipation of the next move by Agent #2. Agent #2 moves to the subject's front left, within a six-foot radius of the subject and says, "Hey!" directed toward the subject. As the subject turns his head ever so lightly to his left, Agent #1 is there and moves unseen and unnoticed by the trickster to seize his left wrist, using the methods explained in this text. Agent #2 draws his weapon stating, "FBI...don't move" and everyone steps back. Agent #3 is now assisting Agent #1 in handcuffing the trickster who is now lying on the ground. The remaining agents set up a perimeter, keeping the crowd back. From the time Agent #2 said, "Hey," two-and-one-half seconds later, the trickster was in handcuffs. We searched him and we found a starter pistol. Of course I asked why he was carrying it. Then I asked him whether he remembered me. He said, "Yes." I told him it took four months but I guess the real bad guy finally showed up at the bus station.

Conclusion

In almost every one of the scenarios presented above, it is essential for at least one agent to have both hands free as the arrest is made. Most often, this is crucial to the successful use of the DRT strategy because it is difficult to walk unnoticed with a drawn gun in your outstretched hands; and it is even more difficult to control a subject with only one hand free. The DRT approach to planned arrests requires well-coordinated teamwork. The "hands-on" agents must be able to trust their teammates to perform their assignments and more if necessary.

In any arrest, no matter how simple it may appear, planning and training are required. However, regardless of the amount of preparation, there will be unpredictable elements. How will the subject react to the loss of freedom? Is the subject a passive individual? Is he combative and prone to violent outbursts or to running away? Are the law enforcement officers confident in their ability to make the arrest? Will they be overly aggressive or overly reserved? Is the subject simply having a bad day, and unwilling to endure another setback? Anything can happen.

The DRT system represents an attempt to achieve predictability and clearly defined procedures in what could be chaotic arrest situations. As I have tried to demonstrate in the preceding discussions, it is sometimes difficult to know what to expect from the subject, simply because of the inherent variability of human nature and of human experience. The components of subject-experienced delayed reaction time (DRT) can be systematically identified, measured, and reliably induced; thereby reducing the unpredictability of the most critical moments during an arrest.

The time that it takes for an agent to exit a van and cover a nine foot expanse is measurable. The reaction time of a human being to a given stimuli (expected or unexpected) is measurable. The circumference of a circle is measurable and so is its radius. Flanks, angles and avenues of escape can be identified. Superiority of numbers, superiority of force and coordinated teamwork can be enhanced through DRT. In this book, the methods by which human reaction time can be reliably prolonged have been quantified and explained at length, and examples of the ways in which these methods can be used to render a subject unable to resist arrest have been given. Training and experience with these methods and strategies can allow law enforcement officers to effectively induce subject DRT, and to make accurate judgments about the moment-to-moment changes in DRT that the subject will then undergo. DRT thus empowers the arrest planners to make more concrete specifications concerning arrest tactics which might be necessary as new situations arise.

The basic tenets of DRT can be the foundations upon which all arrest plans are built. As stated previously, those tenets include:

- Establish a circle of containment;
- Systematically eliminate avenues of escape by reduction of the subject radius using stealth and incremental movements by the arrest team;
- Initiate subject DRT by employing the methods contained in this book;

- Undertake a sudden, dynamic , fluid seizure of the subject instead of a violent or "stand and deliver" seizure; and
- Use planning, coordination, timing, speed and surprise to secure the subject.

The techniques of DRT do not require the subject to make any decisions. Therefore, it is irrelevant whether or not the subject is willing or unwilling to submit, or whether the subject would, under other circumstances, be more prone to have a violent confrontation. DRT thus removes a great deal of this kind of unpredictability from an arrest and provides an effective means of subject control by providing the greatest possible margin of safety for both the pursuers and the pursued. In short, my years of experience with street arrests have convinced me that the optimal levels of safety and effective arrest procedures can be realized through training, coordinated teamwork, and the framework of DRT.

REFERENCES

Adams, R., McKiernan, T., and Remsberg, C. (1980) *Street Survival* Northbook IL: Calibre Press

Applegate, R. (1976). *Kill or get killed* (2nd. Ed.) Boulder, CO: Paladin Press

Cannon, W.B. (1938). *Bodily changes in pain, hunger, fear, and rage* (2nd Ed.), New York: Applegate, Century, Crofts.

Fernandez, M.C. and Vila J. (1989). Sympathetic-parasympathetic mediation of the cardiac defense response in humans. *Biological Psychology* 28, 123-133

Gardner, E. (1976). *Fundamentals of neurology* (6th Ed). Los Angeles Saunders

Kano, Jigoro (1986), *Kodokan Judo* New York: Kodansha International USA

Landis, C., and Hunt, W.A. (1939) *The startle pattern*. New York: Ferrar and Rinehart.

Mussen, P.H. Conger, J.J., Kagan, J. and Huston, C.C. (1990). *Child development and personality* (7th Ed.). New York: Harper-Collins.

Parker, E. (1986). *Infinite insights into Kempo, volume 4.* Los Angeles: Delsby Publications.

Reed, E.S., Ed. (1988) *An ecological approach to the education of behavior.* New York

Remsberg, C. (1986) *The tactical edge*: Northbook IL: Calibre Press

Schiff, W. (1981). *Perception an applied approach*. New York: Houghton Mifflin

Schiff, W. (1981). *The psychology of personal combat*. New York: Praeger.

Stembach, R.A. (1960) A comparative analysis of autonomic responses in startle. *Psychosomatic Medicine*, 22, 204-210.

Turpin, G. (1983) Unconditional reflexes and the autonomic nervous system, in Siddle, D.A.T., (Ed) *Orienting and habituation: perspective in human research*. New York: John Wiley and Sons.

Van Der Graaff, K.M. and Rheas, R.W. (1987). *Human anatomy and physiology*. New York: McGraw.

Watanabe, J. and Abakan, L. (1960). The Secrets of Judo. Rutland, VT: Charles E. Tuttle

Westbrook, A. and Ratty, O. (1970). Aikido and the dynamic sphere Rutland, VT: Charles E. Tuttle.

Tzu, S. (1910). The art of war. Pox Librium Publishing House.

(2002). Webster's New World Dictionary and Thesaurus (2002), (Second ed.). New York: Hungry Minds Inc.

ABOUT THE AUTHOR

Charles E. Williams is founder and CEO of HDI Investigation Service, Inc., a private investigation firm specializing in conducting investigations for criminal defense cases. A graduate of Temple University's School of Business, Charles has built a reputation as an exceptional and highly sought after criminal investigator. After 24 years of exemplary service, Charles retired from the Federal Bureau of Investigation (FBI) where he served as a Special Agent.

Charles' FBI career began in 1983. After graduating from the FBI Academy, he was eventually assigned to the New York City FBI Field Office, where he worked for more than twenty years.

For 14 years, Charles was a member of the prestigious FBI New York City Fugitive Task Force, where he was involved in hundreds of arrests and thousands of interviews. He also attended the FBI undercover agent school and was a member of the New York City FBI Crisis Negotiation Reserve Team; EEO Investigator; Certified FBI Assessor; Certified Street Survival Agent; Community Outreach Specialist; and a General Police Instructor.

Charles worked on a number of high profile FBI cases, including FBI "Top Ten Fugitive" investigation cases. He worked on the Crown Heights Investigation; the World Trade Center bombings (1993): United States Embassy bombing in Tanzania, Africa (1998); and the World Trade Center bombing (September 11, 2001).

As a testimony to his outstanding career in the FBI Charles received a letter of commendation from the United States Attorney General as well as recognition from the United States Attorney's Office for the Eastern District of New York and received twelve letters of commendation from the Director of the FBI. Additionally, he received letters of recognition from the District Attorney of Kings County, Brooklyn, NY; Monmouth County's Prosecutor Office of NJ; the U.S. Army's Criminal Investigation Division (CID); as well as various outside agencies for exemplary performance in the line of duty.

Charles is active in church. He is also a member of Omega Psi Phi fraternity. Hobbies include chess, track, writing, public speaking and exercise. Charles holds a second degree Black Belt in Judo.

Commendations / Special Awards for Exemplary Service:

Director of the FBI, Unlawful Flight to Avoid Prosecution, 1988
Director of the FBI, Unlawful Flight to Avoid Prosecution, 1990
Director of the FBI, Unlawful Flight to Avoid Prosecution, 1991
Director of the FBI, Unlawful Flight to Avoid Prosecution, 1994
Director of the FBI, Unlawful Flight to Avoid Prosecution, 1996
Director of the FBI, Unlawful Flight to Avoid Prosecution, 1996
Office of the County Prosecutor, County of Monmouth, Freehold, NJ, 1990, 1991
Office of the Director of the FBI, Cash Award, Washington, D.C., 1990
Office of the Director of the FBI, Government Reservation Investigation, 1991
San Juan Office, St. Thomas Virgin Islands, Guadeloupe, French West Indies, 1992
Office of the Director of the FBI, World Trade Center, New York, NY, 1993
Office of the Director of the FBI, Tenth Anniversary, Washington, D.C., 1993
Office of the Director of the FBI, Federal Plaza, New York, NY, 1994
District Attorney of Kings County, Municipal Building, Brooklyn, NY, 1995
District Attorney of Kings County, Robert Burke Murder Case, Brooklyn, NY, 1998
Office of the Director of the FBI, Fugitive Task Force, 1995
Office of the Director of the FBI, Bank Robbery Investigation, 1995
Office of the Director of the FBI, Crown Heights/Lemrick Nelson Case, 1995
Office of the Director of the FBI, United States Attorney, Washington, D.C., 1997
District Attorney of Kings County, Law Enforcement Community, Brooklyn, NY, 1997
Office of the Director of the FBI, Crown Heights/Lemrick Nelson Case, 1997
U.S. Attorney Commendation
U.S. Attorney General Janet Reno, Successful Prosecution, Washington, D.C., 1997
U.S. Attorney's Office Eastern District of New York, Recognition award, 2003
U.S. Attorney's Office District of Columbia, letter of Commendation, 1997

Look for these other C.A.R.E. books by **Charles E. Williams**:

An Investigative Way of Life – Expert Interviewing Techniques to Gain Control, Cooperation and Detect Deception

The Song of an Interview – Advanced Techniques to Overcome Subjectivity in an Investigative Interview

www.ingramcontent.com/pod-product-compliance
Lightning Source LLC
Chambersburg PA
CBHW050540270326
41926CB00015B/3321